PEP TALK

A NO BS CONVERSATION ABOUT BOUNDARIES, BLESSINGS, AND BECOMING

❧

FANTAJIA DELISA

CONTENTS

BECOMING

DEDICATION

For our beautiful, chocolate daughters everywhere who need books to be their big sisters.

A NOTE FROM THE AUTHOR

When I became a mother, I had a beautiful, baby girl—and I also had a wake-up call. As soon as I held her, I immediately knew that I needed to make some significant changes in my life. I knew I needed to shift something; in fact, a lot of things. I had someone to provide for, protect, and love. Most importantly, I knew I was responsible for demonstrating the walk of womanhood and to nurture her on her path. Her coming into this world is what set this journey in motion of elevating my life.

I knew her experience needed to be different from mine in every way. As she grows, I can't help but think of the voice I am giving my daughter; something I did not possess at her age. To start this process while she is young is powerful!

Most of us have taught ourselves through trial and error how to be women. We did not have a textbook that outlined the fundamentals of femininity. Most of us never learned how to thrive in our ability to walk in the unknown world. We didn't learn how to stand in our divinity, or how to set standards and boundaries of self-respect. We did not learn how to love ourselves deeply and unapologetically. Some of us did not have the pleasure of seeing what a healthy relationship looks like, let alone, how to manage one. We struggle with knowing when to stay and when to walk away from pain. We do not know how to find peace, beauty, and intentionally create our lives. We want to flourish and bloom into the women that we were created to be but don't know how. Last but not least, we have not learned how to manifest the things we want through picturing. We've given far too much of our power, time and bodies away. We need a book that teaches us how to stand in our truth, and own our magnetic power.

Oh, did I lose you? I hope not; we have a lot to discuss!

I realize now, more than ever, that it is common for women to have shared these same experiences, but it is packaged and sold to us as headlines such as:

How to please your man! Let me show you how to be sexy! Here are five tips to be more beautiful!

WAIT!

All of this is external work; not internal. Where is the guide for internal healing, love, openness, realness and lack of limitations on our lives? Where is the guide that demonstrates true self-love and authentic self-image? By the way, I am not talking about natural hair, no nails, no makeup! I am talking about perfect self-expression.

That is what I want this book to be. A book that guides us through the internal work. I wrote this book for my baby girl and her future friends, but I also wrote it for us because, the truth is, most of us are grown little girls. And in most cases, the little girl in us needs to be healed and made wholeness. With this book, I am going to give my experiences and share my insights on what it means to live a life of constant growth and overall beauty.

It's time to shake some "ish" up. It's time to set some goals and live a life of abundance by making your whole life intentional.

Everything we seek is already created and already in our possession. Your job is to do the required work and embrace the journey.

This is only the beginning of your new lifestyle.

INTRODUCTION

When I was nine years old, I began training to become a dancer. I know that experience, like everything else in my life, wasn't an accident.

At the time, I attended the same public school as most of the kids in my south Los Angeles neighborhood, and had no desire to leave the familiar. I was with the friends and the kids that I'd known for most of my life, and I was as happy as I could be. So, when one of my mother's friends suggested that she consider sending me to a charter school called, The Accelerated School (TAS), I don't think either of us knew how to feel about it.

When my mother mentioned the idea to me, all she told me was that her friend had raved about how good this new school would be for me. The next thing I knew, I was there. *End of story.* But actually, it was more like the beginning.

Fast forward a few weeks later, and I was on the bus to a brand-new world.

I am not knocking public schools at all, but in comparison to the charter school, they felt like the Wild Wild West. My old school was crowded, a little unruly at times, and let's just say, a lot of individual attention and nurturing wasn't typically available. I was one quiet, curious little girl in a sea of children, not knowing that there was anything else out there. You don't know what you don't know.

TAS was different. There were still crowds of kids everywhere, but the difference was a sense of control that even my third-grade mind could comprehend. This wasn't a place that was all play. The standards and expectations were higher.

Instead of starting in the fall semester I was placed in a summer camp run by the school. I was tested and put into a small class of students, most of whom had been in a similar environment all their lives. The struggle to keep up got real, fast. When the end of the school year rolled around, my grades confirmed that my educational level wasn't what it needed to be. I got held back.

It gets better, believe me.

It turned out that not moving forward to the fourth grade was one of the best things that could have happened to me.

Had it not been for TAS, I would never have found my way to my first dance class. My new school had a partnership with a local dance school called, A Place Called Home. It was run by a team of professional dancers and led by two sisters, Monica and Jasmine Guy. Both had trained in New York and had devoted their lives to dance. From theater to film to television, they each had amazing, accomplished careers as dancers, choreographers, producers, and instructors. It was like "A Different World," the hit nineties show, and "School Daze," Spike Lee's iconic movie, both starring Jasmine, had come to life.

There was something—actually many things—about these women that was incredibly special. And it wasn't just how they held themselves as dancers; it was how they held themselves as women.

They were graceful. Confident. Assured about who they were as professionals, and women in the world. Poise and power oozed out of their pores. You could feel it in how they walked into a room. You heard it when they spoke about the books that they'd read, and the people they studied. All of the instructors were beautiful, educated, intelligent, and disciplined women. They'd seen the world and success. They worked hard, but they still had this carefree spirit about them that was so inspiring. These women moved differently from any women that I'd ever met or seen before. They were in their full feminine flow.

Being around those women changed me from the outside in. I learned discipline. I saw what it looked like to be a woman who held her head high and her standards higher. I saw confidence up close. My time with those ladies planted seeds for life lessons that I wasn't fully ready to accept and apply yet, but I "peeped" game. I will always attribute the beginning of my journey to womanhood to this time in my life.

I became a dancer at A Place Called Home. I also became a young woman. But I still had *a lot* of growing up to do.

Most of what I learned was from observation, and very little instruction. Like many girls, I didn't have anyone to teach me how to be a woman. Of course, my mother was present, but she was trying to understand and figure out her life and purpose, as well as support two little girls.

When I got my cycle for the first time, there was no special tea party and the loving period pep talk that Clair Huxtable gave her daughter, Vanessa on, "The Cosby Show." My mother didn't sit me down and talk to me about boys, my body, or much else. I got the same speech that most black and brown girls get.

"Don't get pregnant."

"Don't do drugs."

"Don't hang around people who are about nothing because you will end up being nothing too."

What my mother and the other women in my family did show me was how to make the outside pretty. I assumed that being a woman was all about the superficial things, like getting your nails painted and keeping your hair right. My grandmother came through with the domestic skills, and taught me how to cook and clean and balance a checkbook; core basic survival skills.

But we all find out—usually the hard way—that there is so much more to learn and experience.

Now, I love a beautiful home and a good red lipstick, but our womanhood and femininity are deeper than that. Our mothers and grandmothers taught us how to make it in this world. They demonstrated how to work hard, keep a household up, and how to make sure that our kids never left the house ashy or with their hair uncombed. They taught us how to still look good when we were falling apart. They taught us how to get and keep a man (even if he doesn't deserve you).

But what they didn't teach most of us was how to keep ourselves.

That is what womanhood is really about. Keeping most of ourselves for ourselves. Keeping self-love at the top of our to-do list—always. Keeping ourselves spiritually grounded and constantly connected to a big God. Keeping a bold vision for our lives and living it out.

And that is what brings me to you.

This beautiful journey of womanhood we share is no joke, mainly because no one has taught us how to do this. You're probably a lot like me in that most of what you know about being a woman you've learned through trial and error. Maybe you're like me; you learned some life lessons from watching other women who inspired you. Or you may have had a momma, grandma, auntie, or big sister in your life who taught you a few things, but she missed some steps.

You know there are still some things for you to learn.

I am not here to be your role model, necessarily, but I am here to be the voice in your ear that you've been missing. As women, there are certain things people can't tell us (for fear of hurting our feelings or because they don't know) and things that people won't tell us (sometimes for the same reasons.) I wrote this book to fill in those gaps, and to give you that real advice and real talk that we all need.

You may be in your twenties, thirties, forties, or fifties, and still find yourself struggling with confidence, self-doubt, self-permission, and respect. You are settling. You should be living a much better life, but you are living way below your potential.

It's not that you can't have it. You are stuck in a pattern of bull—. And you need to break it, and break through.

Keep reading.

HOW TO USE THIS BOOK

This book is a process. It is a process of revelation, unlearning, relearning, and *work*.

In Part One, Boundaries, I'll help you to love and elevate yourself in ways that you likely have not before.

In Part Two, Blessings, I'll help you to really get clear about what you desire, get with God, and pray yourself into power and motion.

And in Part Three, Becoming, I'll walk you right up to the woman you will become as you shift your life.

You may be tempted to move through this book quickly, but I want you to take your time. Do the work.

This is a journey. Sit with yourself. Work through it and explore your thoughts. Raise your vibration. Feel the shift and change that is happening.

And then put what you learn in these pages into practice.

If you do, I promise that you will become a different woman.

THE PRE-WORK

ELEVATING YOUR MINDSET

*I*f you've ever worked with a personal trainer or someone to support you in getting your body together, she may have told you that you can't outwork a bad diet. What that means is that you can do all the squats, push-ups, bicep curls, and cardio that you want, but if you don't change what and how you eat, all of that hard work in the gym goes out of the window.

The same is true with the work we do to shift our lives.

We can't outwork a negative mindset. We can read all the self-improvement books. We can get help from the best teachers, mentors, and coaches. We can even temporarily change our behavior, relationships, and space.

But if we don't change our mindset, none of that work will matter. The shift won't stick. If we want real shift, real change, real transformation into our best and highest selves, we must put in that mindset work.

Elevating our mindset is a combination of deciding and doing—in that order. Then repeating that process until the shift sticks.

When I started writing this book, one of the questions I had to think about was when the process of elevating my mindset began for me. The truth is, I'd been doing the work for at least ten years. I didn't realize it at the time, but I was seeking ways to break out of the box that I could have easily been kept in. I was never comfortable in my circumstances (Discomfort is something special. I'll come back to that in a minute).

One of the first big shifts in my life was leaving space and environments that I'd outgrown. In my early twenties, I decided that it was time to move out of my family's house. I wanted my own place. Leaving was about more than just where I showered and slept. I wanted peace; I complete control over my physical and mental space. I wanted different energy. I wanted a completely different life than what 52nd and Broadway could offer me at the time. I decided that it was time to create the lifestyle I thought I wanted as a young woman.

I had to get rooted in elevation.

I needed to get in my mind that I was a woman who lived a certain way. I had to raise my vibration to the level of a woman who lived where and how she wanted to live. I had to know what was possible for myself, and unlearn everything that I'd been taught and told about the fear and limitation that could keep me where I no longer wanted or needed to be.

There was a lot of work and hard moments associated with the sacrifices to be made, but it was necessary. And it set my life in motion. That move created a permanent pattern of being able to shift in my life. When I had my daughter, about six years ago, I felt the squeeze to shift again. I needed to create a new life for her, and become the next level, the next version of myself, to give her everything that I wanted her to have. But unlike the young girl moving out on her own for the first time, I didn't stumble into the shift—I was intentional about it.

"Okay, Fantajia. It's time. Do what you need to do." (That's me talking to myself)

What I needed to do was elevate my mindset, and put my shift in motion in every way. That shift was focused on my finances and status. I wanted to earn more. So, I became that woman, and was soon the youngest senior manager in my company. I wanted to rebrand my business, so I redirected my energies and created the new shift in my business. The elevation process now includes my health. I want to be the woman who runs multiple businesses, writes and publishes best-selling books, and tours the country inspiring and motivating women. I need the energy to flow from business to business, to book signings, to speaking engagements. It will be impossible for me to do all of this if I am moving like a slug and don't have the energy. Health equals wealth, and to become a woman who earns at a higher level, I have to get my body into the healthiest state in which it's ever been.

Increasing income. Changing cities. Up-leveling careers. Losing weight. Regardless of what shift needs to happen, it comes back to elevating my mindset.

Decide and Do. This is the process I put into play whenever it is time for me to elevate and shift.

You can do the same. So, Let's jump right in and begin to break this concept down.

1. **Decide what needs to be different for you.** Make the decision to do, be, and have more. Decide to have a different life and experience; to be a different woman in some way. You have the control and the power to change any circumstance in your life.

2. **Decide exactly where you are going.** You need to get clear on what you want to change. Do you want to move? Then get clear on the neighborhood in which you'd like to live. Do you want to get more fit and in shape? Then get clear on how you want to feel, and what that endgame looks like. Think about it like this: If you wanted a Chanel bag, and you walk into a mall that you've never been to before, would you just randomly wander through the mall until you bump into the Chanel store, or would you use the directory to find exactly where that store is? Your shift has a location and definitive destination. Be clear on what that is so you know it when you see it.

3. **Do the things.** Get rooted in the vision. Raise yourself to a vibration level that aligns with your shift. Change your

current thoughts, environment, and behavior. Fill your ears with positive words of affirmation and put them everywhere around you. If people in your life have to go, cut them loose. Stop going into low-end stores and restaurants if you want a luxury lifestyle. If you need to increase your income, then find a better paying job or start the side hustle. If you need to change your diet and eat healthier foods, do it. This is the work required to create what you desire. Do you want this? Then work for it.

4. **Do the assessment.** Constantly check in with yourself to be sure you are moving in the direction of your destination. If you get off course, then make the required adjustments. Refer to Step 3 to help you get back on track.

AND THIS IS A BONUS—

Live the reality. As you move, maintain the energy of yes. No doubt. No desperation. Simply ridiculous belief and knowing that what you have decided to have what is yours. It's happening. Show up in every space as if it already has.

DISCOMFORT IS YOUR SHIFT SIGNAL

Do you remember when I mentioned being uncomfortable in my circumstances and how that discomfort was a sign that I needed to shift?

I was a young twentysomething woman who wanted her own apartment because I was uncomfortable in South Central Los Angeles. I was a young mother who wanted her daughter in a great school but couldn't afford it. My discomfort started speaking to me, telling me that it was time. I listened.

I have a feeling that you know exactly what I am talking about. You are uncomfortable with where you are in your life.

That discomfort could be with the home you live in, the amount of weight that you're carrying on your body, or the amount of money in your bank account. Your circumstances and your life are speaking to you right now.

Are you listening?

As women, especially as black and brown women, we tend to put our discomfort on mute. For many of us, struggling, suffering, and settling is in our DNA. So, it becomes a way of life. We accept the things that we believe we cannot change. But I am here to tell you that you can change. Frustration, fear, sadness, and struggle, does not have to be your reality. Stop denying your desires and dreams. If you want something, go get it.

I know you've heard the saying, "You can run, but you can't hide." This is so true when it comes to what you want. You can tell yourself that you can make do with your current situation all you want to but feelings don't lie. Every time you look at other women who live how you want to live, you feel that jealousy creeping up whenever you see them. Listen, jealousy is a real thing. We all feel it. It's okay. That discomfort is your signal to level up

Two signs that it's time to shift:

1. **You are uncomfortable in your current circumstances.**
2. **You can see yourself somewhere else.**

Whenever these come up for you consistently, listen. *Move.* You know when you don't belong where you are anymore. You know what you know.

Something else that I want to make clear: the shift process is also one of discomfort.

The sacrifice that is required to change your life *hurts*. Giving up something to have something more is not a game. You will want to quit. You will want to go back to where it's comfortable: The job you know. The man you know. The friends you know. The food you know. All of the behaviors, people, and environments you know are no longer healthy, but their familiarity feels safe to you. And the fearful thinking that fills your head will tell you to stay there.

THIS IS where the decision comes in.

What do you want? Do you want it bad enough to do differently? Do you want it more than you are afraid of it? If the answer is, "yes," then the discomfort is a small price to pay to achieve success.

MORE PRACTICES FOR ELEVATING
YOUR MINDSET

As you are moving through this journey, you may have to prime your mind again and again to stay in the zone, and in the alignment of what you are shifting into. Here are some of my go-to practices for keeping my vibration high:

- **Know that it is possible.** This one was major for me in the beginning of my journey. As a girl who wanted a better life I had to work hard to up-level my thinking around what *I* could have and do. The more that I put myself through the Decide/Do process and stepped into the life I wanted my sense of self-worth transformed. I became the woman who deserved everything that I desired.

Take the limits off your thinking. Get down in your spirit and your subconscious that everything you want is available to you. I know that you know a woman who has the life, the body, the career, the money that you want. If she can have it, why can't you?

- **Having more is not a bad thing.** This goes hand-in-hand with knowing that whatever you want is possible. Unlearn the belief that there is a problem with having more.

Many of us come from environments where we are taught that there is something wrong with having more. We grow up hearing negative thoughts such as "Money doesn't grow on trees," "People who have money are assholes," or that rich people are greedy. We don't realize how hearing these ideas, beliefs, and lies over and over again for years has seeped into our psyche. We have all of these blocks, beliefs, and fears around earning and having more, but don't understand why. This is why—the broken record that has been playing in our minds for years.

Here's the truth, and I want you to hear me so you can heal: **nothing you want is wrong** - a different life; a different home; a different man; more money and financial flow. None of these things are wrong. The more money you have, the more you can do. Cash creates choices. You should want the best for yourself. Whatever that looks like is up to you.

- **Open yourself up to receiving.** Desire is one of the powerful seeds that God gives us as women. Your heart, your spirit, your intuition does not lie. So, since you feel it, and you can see yourself in a different life and space, it must be meant to be. You are meant to be. Let what comes to you come. It may be tomorrow or two years from now, but it's coming. Be ready.

- **Change your surroundings.** I mentioned this before, but I'll say it again. As you are shifting and elevating your life, look around you, take inventory, and remove what isn't serving you. Put yourself in the vibration level to be able to make shifts happen. Shake some "ish" up.

What have you been doing that is contrary and out of alignment with what you want? Those are the things you need to change. Change spaces. Change what you read and listen to. Change people (you can't actually change people, but you can swap them out for others who work with your desires and not against them). Take control of your environment. Require that everything around you rise higher and watch how those changes elevate everything in your life.

- **Know that you are the good thing.** We all have adjustments that we need to make.
- **You are already worthy. I want you to hear me:** yes, you are taking action and shifting towards something new. But the woman you are today is a woman who deserves everything in the world. Once you know that, you can put the practices and principles to work in order to have it.

KEEP MOVING, KEEP CORRECTING

$\mathcal{J}$f you haven't noticed yet, I use the word "journey" a lot so far. This is very intentional. What I want you to remember is that this work you are preparing to do is a process. You are shifting. You are changing. You are evolving. And you are learning, unlearning, and relearning lessons, beliefs, and behaviors that will change as you do.

Womanhood is being willing to constantly correct. To reset. To learn and keep learning. Life and experience will teach you.

You can have everything you want now, and then one day you will look at yourself in the mirror and say, "Girl, it's time for more." There will always be new levels to attain. And those new levels will require you to become a different woman each time.

Be willing to die to the old you so that you can keep living.

BOUNDARIES

You have set standards for how you want to be treated and what you expect from yourself and for yourself. – Iyanla Vanzant

THE BEAUTY OF BOUNDARIES

I want you to take a second and think about the most powerful woman that you know. You may not have a relationship with her, but from a distance you've watched how she moves. You can tell, even if you have never had a conversation with her, that she says what she means and means what she says. She appears to make decisions about herself and her life with ease.

She is in alignment with, and guided by something bigger than herself. She stands and speaks up for herself. She is strong and firm, but still feminine. She is confident and classy. She has healthy relationships. She exudes an energy of happiness, love, and light.

She seems to have whatever she needs—and desires.

Do you see her? Do you feel her? Good. I want you to hold the vision of that woman in your mind for a minute.

Now, let's paint a different picture. Think about the woman that you've met who is the exact opposite of the woman you just envisioned.

This is a woman who radiates insecurity. She is quiet. Not in a I'll-speak-when-I-have-something-to-say way, but more of a I'd-rather-shrink-than-be-heard kinda way. She takes what comes. She is incredibly talented, but she is overworked and underpaid. In her relationships, she pours plenty out, but takes in very little. She tolerates the man who constantly gets caught cheating, who humiliates her by calling her outside of her name, or worse, puts his hands on her. She is the woman who settles and you see it. She is the woman you've always vowed to never become-even if you've looked up to her-and yet, you have

We could guess that these two women's lives and experiences are so drastically different for many reasons. Age. Ambition. Luck. Looks. And all of these things are possible. But there is something else, something bigger, that sets these women apart from one another.

Boundaries.

Let me tell you why.

Every woman's life is defined by the boundaries that she has or does not have. Boundaries are the baseline and foundation for everything we do. Boundaries direct day-to-day decisions. Boundaries define what you keep out or allow in your life.

Boundaries set standards and expectations.

Boundaries create control over your life and your response to it.

Boundaries create confidence.

And once set, boundaries are lines that should never be crossed by anyone—including yourself.

I am sure you've heard a lot of conversation about the need for boundaries in your life, particularly in your relationships. And that is definitely true. Your boundaries determine how people show up at the door of your life—family, friends, lovers, coworkers—and what they are allowed to do once they arrive.

Women with clear, defined boundaries require respect.

Women with boundaries know their worth and what they deserve.

So, they are not clinging to men who only call when it's convenient or girlfriends who are constantly making emotional withdrawals from the friendship without any deposits. At work or in their businesses, they seek and get salaries that align with their value and expertise. They speak up when someone crosses their line.

Women with boundaries have goals.

So, they invest in their development—physically, spiritually, mentally, and financially.

Women with boundaries have set a standard for themselves and their lives, and are committed to being their highest and best selves.

So, they make their self-care and happiness a priority. Their time at the gym or facials aren't skipped to serve other people-even those they love. Their morning time with God is uninterrupted. They love themselves, and then everybody else.

Women with boundaries are happy, confident, and *#unbothered* as a result of the daily decisions they make to choose themselves. When your boundaries are set, you feel completely powerful and in control of your life. You can flow through life without having to constantly stress and figure out what's right for you and what's not. You aren't taking a passive approach to your life where you accept whoever and whatever comes.

Your boundaries are your contract with yourself to do what you need to do for you. And I want you to sign, seal, and deliver it—to yourself and everyone else in your life.

Do you mind if I get spiritual for a minute?

We've talked about the practical and tactical need for boundaries; and, don't worry because we're not done. But boundaries are, first and foremost, divine. God is a God of order, and order is First Law. God has defined an order and a flow for everything in our lives. Our boundaries are an extension of God. They are our moral compass and our guide.

WHERE YOUR BOUNDARIES ARE
BROKEN

If I were your let-me-be-really-straight-up-with-you homegirl (which I actually am) and you asked me, "Fantajia, where do you think I need boundaries in my life?" my response would be simple: "Everywhere".

This sentence is almost a word for word repeat of what you've stated separately. This small paragraph is superfluous; it can be taken out.

Whenever we feel a lack of control of what is happening in our lives and our day-to-day experiences, it's a sign that we need to create or reevaluate our boundaries. Where have we slipped up? What have we allowed? Where have we forgotten who we are?

Like many women, boundary-setting has been trial and error for me. It's a practice on which I still work. No one teaches us about boundaries and why they are so necessary. I was well into my twenties when I started to notice patterns in my life with myself and my relationships that no longer felt good to me. I was sad, frustrated, disappointed, and disrespected constantly.

Even with all that frustration and drama, I didn't change right away. It was a slow, gradual process where I started giving myself more permission and more voice in my life. I didn't know any better. I didn't have a woman in my life to saw me and my struggles, and wanted to be my "get-it-together" guide.

A bigger part of my issue was that I was conditioned that love was supposed to hurt. I was conditioned to believe that Black women were supposed to be muted at work. So why would I believe that I was supposed to have anything different?

But none of that is an excuse now to not live differently and demand more. I had to own my stuff.

Once I got tired of being tired, I started to break through the limited thinking and conditioning that kept me from taking control of my life in the way which I needed. I decided the standards I needed to set, the boundaries that I needed to put in place, and what Fantajia needed to be good. The result was less drama, less distractions, and less noise in my life.

Now, can I be 100 percent honest with you?

I don't have this boundary-setting thing on lock completely.

This has been a journey for me, and it will be for you too. The standards and boundaries you set for yourself will change and evolve as you do. But you can start today, right where you are.

So how do you know if your boundaries are out of sync with who you are? Let me share a few signs:

You don't need this because it's already clear to the reader that this is about herself.

- You are often frustrated with where you are in life.
- You feel out of alignment with your values and how you want to live and love.
- You say you want one thing, but you do something else.
- You self-sabotage (whenever you get momentum towards your goals, you do something to f@#k it up.
- Your actions and your words are misaligned with your wants.
- You don't feel good about yourself.
- You are always busy, but never making any progress in your life.

When it comes to others:

- You are passive.
- You don't know how to communicate with people who upset you.
- You don't hold people accountable when they hurt you.
- You feel used and run over.
- You feel overextended.
- You are always giving time and energy into people and places that aren't returning the favor.
- You are constantly putting everything and everyone else before yourself.
- You feel like you are constantly bending over backwards, emotionally twisting and turning, to get along with people.
- You are struggling to fit in a space—a job, a business, a friendship—that doesn't feel in alignment with who you are.

Your feelings are a temperature gauge that will tell you *exactly* what needs to change. If you were nodding your head to any of those indicators above, then listen to that. Feel that.

Whatever your life looks like, however you feel in your relationships, it means something. Especially if it doesn't feel good.

Your inner feelings need to become your outer boundaries.

Let's get that together.

BUT FIRST, SOME STANDARDS

You may have noticed that I speak about boundaries and standards in the same conversation, and that is because once you have one (standard) you have the other (boundary). Your boundaries become clearer, easier, and elevated when you know what you want and need for yourself.

I've found that a lack of standards is a source of a lot of drama, confusion, and noise in our lives.

Show me a woman who is struggling with her self-esteem, confidence, and respect in her relationships, and I will show you a woman with no standards for herself.

Once you have your standards set, you have something to measure against.

The beginning of this sentence does not make good sense. Here is an option: You can begin assessing every area of your life with one question: "Is this relationship/situation/conversation/behavior meeting my standards?" Standards make situations less blurry and complicated. They remind you of who you are, and provide you with the self-respect required to move on when what you want and need is no longer available. Standards help you shift forward.

And let me say this: you don't have to be ashamed for not getting this right. That is learned behavior taught by the people around you, and reinforced by the world. Because of this conditioning, you have not known that you deserved more. If that was not your experience, it's okay. Most of us have a mind to work when start to understand that we must change how we see ourselves. And then it takes practice. It takes time. And it takes acceptance of who and where we are. We have to accept responsibility for ourselves, our decisions, and how we want to live moving forward. That is all up to us.

Setting standards is the ultimate gift of self-love that you give yourself. We read blogs and articles about pampering our bodies and doing all the lovely beauty rituals that make us look good. I love the feminine things too, and taking care of your body and appearance is important. We feel good when we look good. We feel strong and confident when we strut down the street with glowing skin and pretty curls. But do you know where real confidence comes from?

Standards and control over your life. The control over what you give away and what you keep for yourself. Self-respect. And choosing yourself.

That is confidence, ladies. That is feminine power.

Standards are self-love in practice and in motion.

As you begin to think about the standards you need to create in your life, I want you to do some soul-searching. Here are three important questions for you to think about and answer:

- **Who am I?** Think about the woman you know you were created to be. Who is she?
- **What am I doing?** Next, take an honest look at your life. What are your habits and behaviors? What relationships and situations are you in right now? What cycles are repeating in your life? What conversations are you continuously having with yourself and others? How do you feel about them? Do you feel good? Do you feel proud? Happy? Satisfied? Or do you feel unhappy? Do you feel unfulfilled? Unsuccessful?
- **Where am I going?** Lastly, what do you want for yourself?

What are your goals for your life? What type of relationships do you want, romantic, friendships, and business? When you look in the mirror, what do you want to see? As you move through your life, how do you want to feel?

Do you see any disconnects between your responses? Do you see how what you are doing, accepting, and allowing is out of alignment with who you are and where you are going?

With this clarity around where you need new or higher standards, let's establish what our standards will look like from today forward.

STANDARDS AND COMMITMENTS

Ask yourself, "What do *I* want?" Answer that question for yourself.

Now that you know what you want, what are you committed to, to achieve it? Going forward, you have to be committed to living, speaking, acting, thinking and overall doing everything in your life to reflect what it is you are calling forth.

While you are in manifestation mode and recreating your standards, boundaries and new commitments to yourself, be quiet about them. You do not need to make an announcement of what you are doing. Use this time to sharpen your words.

Here is a tip:

"A fool uttereth all his mind: but a wise (wo)man keepeth it in till afterwards" – Proverbs 29:11

Before we start anything, let's start the conversation with God. Use this space to address where you have lowered your standards. This is where you forgive and make new commitments with yourself and God.

USE this space to let your mind, heart and soul pour and flow.

Now that we have laid it at the altar, write down three areas that you're going to focus on changing.

1.

2.

3.

WRITE down what your NEW commitments are.

There you have it. The foundation of the new you. Please pause and take in three deep breaths. Inhale all the goodness you feel. Exhale all the lack you no longer desire. Sit with that.

The work that you've just done will now be the guide for the woman you are from this day forward. I hope that as you are doing this work, that you begin to feel something. I want you to feel yourself shifting into a new woman, a better woman, than you were before. I want you to feel more confident, stronger, more determined to meet the standards that you've set for yourself.

You are a woman who is worthy of the best; you are worthy of respect. You are a woman who loves herself so much that she refuses to settle for anything less than what she deserves. You are a woman who chooses herself.

Congratulations, sis. You just set a new bar for your life.

YOUR STANDARDS ARE NON-NEGOTIABLE

C&

*A*s hard as it was to get clear on the new standards you have set for yourself, that was just the beginning. Enforcing these standards with others, and holding yourself to them is work too.

Once you set standards for yourself, they will be tested. You'll get lax with yourself. You'll get comfortable. You'll grow and mature and forget to adjust your standards to reflect the new level of life that you've reached. You'll meet people, let them into your life, and realize that you are making allowances for them and lowering your standards in hopes that they will rise to meet them.

Again, I cannot stress enough that how you treat, love, and respect yourself says so much. What you allow tells everyone who steps to you what your standards are. But we'll get to other people in a minute; let's stay focused on you right now. Because before we can hold other people accountable for how they show up in our lives, we have to account for our own behaviors.

So, what is within *your* control? What standards have you set for yourself that only require your participation and commitment?

Your standards are those ever-present personal reminders of what you need to do and be for you. Write them in your mind so that you don't forget or them. They will always bring you back to who you are.

Whenever I think about standards, I go back to my dancing days.

The techniques and the way we were taught to hold our bodies and to move were standards for all dancers to follow. When I was on stage, if I did not do what I was taught, my body wouldn't do what it was supposed to do. I always had a set of standards I could fall back on to figure out where I went wrong. Then I could make the proper adjustment.

Right now, I want a better body. When I am in lose weight, get healthy mode, I don't eat after 8 p.m. because I know late-night eating slows down my metabolism. I eat healthy foods throughout the day. If my guy came over to my place and wanted to have a late dinner, my answer would be an easy "no."

My health and reaching my goals are non-negotiables for me. I refuse to allow anything or anyone to get in the way of that. If you are having trouble creating boundaries for yourself, then use the following for inspiration. These are some that I have created for myself. These things that are not up for negotiation:

- I will not be surrounded by people or environments that do not inspire, uplift me or that will dull my light.
- I will not have friends around me that keep me small minded or make me feel uncomfortable about me being me. I will show up in the world as myself. I will remove myself from situations requiring me to do otherwise.
- I am committed to choosing me first.
- I am committed to ensuring to keep my cup full and anyone that drains it is NOT my people.

This mind shift has spilled over into my business, my relationships, family and how I show up in the world.

What are your non-negotiable standards?

If you are a woman who is successful, healthy, and inspiring to others, those are your standards.

If you are always on time and you require others to be also, that is a standard.

If your minimum salary has to be $80,000 for you to live how you want to live, that is a standard.

If you only date men who have the time and money to take you on weekly dates, that is a standard.

If you don't date married men, that is a standard.

There is no right or wrong answer here. You get to decide what your standards are. Don't be afraid to set them however you like.

This is your life. Design and define it. Control it. Live it.

LIFE IS A GAME. MAKE YOUR RULES

*R*emember this: life is a game. It's not a game of perfection, but of constant correction. In this game, your standards and boundaries for others are your rules.

You know that you have been playing this game without the right rules. You have allowed everyone else around you to decide the rules for your game. That is why it's been such a struggle. The drama in your life is not you—it's that you have been playing a game without rules. So, you feel as if you have been getting played. We're not playing *that* game anymore. You are making your rules.

But—

You are constantly learning more about the woman you are and who you want to be, so leave room to correct. Leave room to do better as you know better, as Maya Angelou taught us. Leave room to reevaluate and readjust your standards. Give yourself grace as you figure this thing out.

BOUNDARIES IS A VERB

Once you've become clear on your personal standards and how you need to move with and for yourself, it's time to do the work to define how you will move with other people. Let's get into those boundaries.

If it has not sunk in yet, boundaries are not just words we say. They are actions that we *do*. Boundaries are verbs. They are actions. And they are intentional.

Boundaries are not something that you can leave to chance. I've made the mistake, and trust me, this is not the area to neglect. Before I learned how to establish boundaries in my life, I endured and suffered from situations I had no business experiencing. l I just thought good things would happen as a natural result of me treating people well. I was so wrong. *We* are so wrong. WRONG! Some things have to be a hard NO!

Often, we avoid boundaries because we don't want the discomfort that comes with them. We are protecting other people's emotions and feelings. We want to allay or pacify any hurt feelings from others that may come as a result of the boundaries we set for ourselves. And, I am about to go there. Are you ready? We are afraid they will abandon us.

Yes, I said it. We do not set boundaries because of our own internal feelings of rejection

All of this typically comes down to one thing—fear.

Fear that we'll get fired from our jobs or dropped by clients, causing loss of income. Fear that those with whom we are involved will argue and pushback, causing friction in the relationship. Fear that our children will think we're mean parents. Fear that people will walk away, causing heartbreak and loneliness. Fear that you will stand alone because you couldn't get with their program.

These are all valid reasons to fear. And I am going to keep it all the way real with you-these things may happen. Your boundaries will create conflict. You will take a loss in some form or another.

But your standards of self-love and self-respect, are virtuous and priceless. Any discomfort that you feel a small price to pay. That discomfort is nothing in comparison to freedom. It's not up for discussion. It is what it is. If others cannot get with that program, those are not your tribe. People will rise to the occasion or fall off of your vibration.

When they do, let them.

And let me say this— people leaving your life is a part of the process. Don't take this as rejection, or an indication that your standards are too high, or your boundaries are too strict. Trust yourself enough to know when your boundaries have become a wall or a prison. Trust your Intuition. Some people are seasonal, and that's ok. You will be okay.

Here is a litmus test:

1. Try this instead: Do you measure up to the standards and boundaries you have set for yourself, and expect others to meet? Keep your voice active. Try to avoid passive voice as much as possible.

2. Do you give what you are asking to receive?

3. Do the people around you match your frequency and flow? Do they encourage you to raise yours?

The goal is to achieve and experience meaningful, healthier, higher vibrating relationships that make you feel good, safe, and supported. You want to attract like-minded people and opportunities that are abundant, and provide for you well. There is absolutely nothing wrong with that. All of these will come when you are bold enough to stand up for yourself and declare to the world what you want, need and desire.

Your time, your energy, your heart and money—anything that is of value and important to you need guidelines so that you manage all of it well. Like a fence, your boundaries are meant to protect these pieces of you; not to restrict you from loving, living, giving, earning, and finding happiness. Boundaries should make room for all of those things to flow to you and allow you to feel good in the process.

I've mentioned this, but the confidence that comes with standards and boundaries is powerful.

Confidence is like your signature scent. It draws the right people and things to you. It allows for your presence to be felt as soon as you walk in the room. The woman who means what she says. The woman who plays no games. The woman who takes no shit. To me, the most beautiful part about this process is that it doesn't have to be a negative thing. You can be the one that person that everyone loves to be around, wants to be around, and adores.

Do not shrink yourself or shy away from doing hard things in your life, such as establishing boundaries. This is a journey. I've said this before. It is not about perfection. This journey is about constant correction. There is no wrong or right way to go about this.

Remember, this is coming from a place of I wish I knew then, what I am learning to understand now. I wish someone spoke to me about boundaries. It's not always easy. This chapter provides space for reflective thought; a place where you ask yourself where you are this journey. If you find you're not on the desired path, reevaluate your boundaries and change it.

THE BOUNDARY BLUEPRINT

*a*s you begin this boundary work, you may be wondering how to do it, what your boundaries should look like, and where to start. And please remember, during this process and time, be patient with yourself.

Your boundaries are personal to you, your needs, and your comfort levels. In the sections to come, I am going to go a little deeper on some of my own boundaries and share how I created them and why.

When it comes to boundaries, there is a blueprint that I follow that you can use as general guidelines for creating your own boundaries:

1. **Boundaries should align with your moral compass.** At this point in your life, you know what your values are. Some relate to God, church, and your spiritual beliefs. Others relate to your family and how you were raised. Some you've adopted by observing others, and adopting their beliefs as your own. The morals and values that feel good and correct to you should define and guide your boundaries. Don't allow people to do things to you or around you that compromise what is right for you.

2. **Boundaries change as you do.** Boundaries will evolve as you do. As you become more self-confident, you gain more wisdom and experience. This will help you decide what boundaries you need.

3. **Boundaries are trial and error.** You will set some boundaries, try them out, and find that you need stronger ones. Or you might find that you need to loosen them up a bit. You'll know as you grow.

4. **Boundaries can vary from person to person.** The boundaries that you have for your child will be different than the boundaries that you have for co-workers. Boundaries are driven by the closeness and intimacy of the relationship.

5. **Boundaries are for every area of your life.** Your boundaries may differ from person to person, but everywhere that you interact with people, boundaries are required.

I've set a standard that I will live my life by telling the truth, nothing but the truth, so help me God. In the spirit of full transparency, I still work at establishing boundaries when necessary. There are some that are completely clear and easy for me to stick to. With others, I have to be self-conscious and aware, and resist the urge to compromise myself so I don't end up regretting my actions.

I am far better than I used to be, but in some areas of my life are still a work in progress. There are areas I still don't get right one hundred percent of the time. I trip up; sometimes, I make mistakes. But I actively practice what I am sharing you. It is a game of constant correction. I adjust my rules, correct myself, and move on.

TEACH PEOPLE HOW TO TREAT YOU

⁂

I will never forget the day I learned this concept. I allowed someone to get too close to me, too fast because I was vague in all of my responses to her push to want to know me. I did not want to hurt her feelings, so I pacified her unwelcomed behaviors. She posed as a friend, but she had other motives. She showed up to events to which I never invited her. She tried to connect with the people in my social circle behind my back to get more information about me. The final straw? She attempted to expose me at my place of work. I learned not to match energy. I maintain mine and align, I should have set my boundaries from the beginning, but I didn't. Never say "maybe" when you really mean "no". I told myself going forward, I will be clear; my no means no.

Boundaries are an expression of your standards and expectations. "You teach people how to treat you." First stated by Dr. Phil, and since appropriated by others including Oprah, it is a profound truth; one to keep close to your heart. This, ladies, is gold. We can't continue to move through life expecting people to show up already knowing our rules for how we are to be treated. Their first interactions with us will be a direct reflection of how we care for ourselves. So, it is important that others see that we hold ourselves in high esteem and that our boundaries show how we feel about ourselves. This sets the tone for others on how they should deal with us.

And there is a formula for this:

What you do + what you say and/or how you treat others = how people treat you and/or how they communicate with you + how they show up in your life.

Reflection.

Some might ask, "Fantajia, are you're telling me that if I am being abused, I asked for that?"

No. I'm simply saying that you *accept* it.

Secondly, there is what you allow others to do to you. People can tell a lot about what you will tolerate based on your behavior, especially staying silent when they mistreat you.

If you haven't been treated well by someone, check what you've taught them. Have you demonstrated self-respect and high standards? Have you checked the person who treated you poorly?

If you have some teaching to do in your life, it's okay. I am here to help.

BOUNDARIES IN REAL LIFE

*O*kay, so we've talked a lot about what boundaries should look like in theory. Now let's see what they look like in practice. I'll go first. Here are some of the boundaries that I have in place today:
Work.

At work, I have a boundary around my energy and the relationships I've established with my employees. I do not allow anyone on my team to come to me with problems without a solution.

This particular boundary was inspired by a manager I had years ago. Whenever I would barge into his office to vent, he would tell me, "Don't put your monkey on my back." What he meant by that was, don't bring me your issues and problems.

I've taken that same position with my staff. I am here to support and help them work through an issue, but I will not allow them to throw their issues on me.

I also do not have conversations about my personal life with my coworkers. Whew, child! You think they are your friends? NOPE! Keep balance by keeping that area separated.

To add to this, I prefer they do not as well. I made the mistake once or twice in allowing people to vent. The problem is you have to hold their emotions for them and that is not fair to you. Do not allow people to dump their emotions on you. It becomes too heavy to carry. No one should be forced to hold someone else's secrets.

Love.

In my intimate relationships with men, I've set specific boundaries that apply to everyone:

You will not interrupt my peace. PERIOD.

I have fallen short in this area in my life. I have not made good decisions with men.

This area has tested me the most.

However, I've learned that, number one, my past cannot touch me. I have forgiven myself for not having boundaries, but check this out; I was never taught that! Therefore, I am easy on myself about that now. I have come to understand, every past relationship was a mirror of where I mentally was at that time. I will dive into this deeper shortly.

As women, our boundaries with men can be hard to establish. Men get in our lives, under our skin and confidence, and in our heart space. Men can reopen unhealed emotional wounds. And because of this, it can be more difficult to establish boundaries with men—at first.

But before we can teach them how to treat us, we may have to learn a lot of hard lessons about ourselves.

MEN MAY BE YOUR MIRROR

*W*hen you start healing from wounds can provide us with the opportunity to look back on the relationship from which we've just come. Oftentimes, relationship with a man is like a mirror; it reflects everything we are at the time of our involvement with that person.

While in my studies, I found the courage to look at every relationship that I'd ever been in; I could see the cycles of abuse. I'd been in one abusive relationship after another. I was on an emotional rollercoaster. There was verbal abuse, physical abuse and/or men who were not emotionally available.

I sort of grew up in a verbally abusive and violent home. I say sort of because I was barely, home! From school I went to dance class, and then I tended to my studies. I really didn't pay too much attention. But I do recall my father and I colliding over his continual verbal abuse towards my mother. I had had enough of hearing the B word slung all over the place. Now mind you, I was a Daddy's girl up until where I started to see what was really happening in my home. The stress my mother was experiencing and the lack of support, I would assume. My father had never chastised me in my life. He never directly hurt me, but I saw how he handled my mother, and it hurt. Right before I moved out, I made this comment to him:

"You have girls! We will be women. And you sat here and taught us that it is acceptable for a man to treat us like this. Fucking fool!" The next day, I moved out. I hurt my Mother because I stopped coming by. I told her, "If you stay with this clown, you're a clown. The fact that he is our Daddy isn't a good enough excuse for me any longer. The way I see it, more damage has been done."

Full disclosure, I forgave my mother because she was doing her best and wanted her little girls to grow up with their dad in home. She gave what she thought was important. And I respect that. I've learned that before my mother was my mom, she was a young woman trying to figure this whole thing out too.

I say all of that to say, my father was my mother's mirror. He met her where she was and held her there.

With that being my only road map at the time, I ran from home to escape the nonsense, and it still showed up in my next relationship. What I thought I was running from, was showing up in my life because I did not acknowledge it, therefore, I could not heal from it. I knew I didn't want to be the woman who let a man put his hands on her or call her out of her name. But I did not know to set standards. (Sounds hella crazy right?) I am serious, and I am sure you have been through similar times. Gray areas = no boundaries!

It took years of rooting this out through therapy, hiring life coaches, and so much more to face the real problems in this area. My standards and boundaries are set and are clearer, but remember, this is a constant area of improvement. I will not stand before you and claim a false reality. Again, it's not about perfection. It's about continuous correction. Now, I do have a standard on how men handle me. I have learned that my boundaries are a reflection of my self-value. My request to you is that you handle your boundaries as a treasure to yourself and allow no one to rob that space.

You decide what makes you comfortable, but here's what I want you to learn from me.

As women, we often want to blame men for how they treat us. Do

48

they have a responsibility for the disrespect, the cheating, and the lies? Sure, they do.

But as grown women, we have to accept responsibility for what we've allowed too. We have to own where our standards and confidence were at such a low level that we became a wide-open door for a man like that to walk through.

Iyanla Vanzant has a powerful quote:

"It's not that you chose him. It's that you allowed him to stay."

We get caught up in questioning why we attract certain types of men. But the bigger question is, once we see that they are not able to meet our standards or respect our boundaries, why do we allow them to stay?

Men are attracted to the standards that we set. If we have low or no standards, we call men to us who are the same, and who, in turn, devalue and mistreat us. But when we the bar high, the experience is usually the opposite. We draw men who handle and treat us well.

Men are our mirrors.

When you look in the mirror of the men in your past or present, what woman do you see? Is she secure in herself? Does she demand respect? Or does she allow men to run over and disrespect her?

If what you are seeing is negative, go deeper with that. Explore why you've settled. Is it fear or rejection? Is it abandonment? Is it a need for love and attention that you aren't getting somewhere else? Spend some time in this space. Resist the urge to run from the feelings and get to the root. If you are in between relationships, and you've been unhappy with the men from your past, now is the time to do this healing work.

Because here's the truth:

You can't love others if you don't love yourself, and you can't love others more than yourself.

Too often as women, we are far more focused on who loves us, and what we need to do to get and keep that love, than we are on loving ourselves. We toss our standards and our boundaries aside in the name of love.

But now we're shifting that. We are taking the time to get with, and keep, *ourselves*. We're learning to love ourselves.

I want you to start loving yourself more than you ever have before.

When you love yourself, you hold yourself to a higher standard for everything else in your life, including men. You won't tolerate anything less than you deserve.

Do this work so that the next mirror you meet reflects the woman you know you are—beautiful, divine, and worthy.

BOUNDARIES ARE MEANT FOR YOUR LIPS TO SAY (AND THEIR EARS TO HEAR)

OUR BOUNDARIES ARE meaningless if no one knows about them but us. We have to make them known; we have to verbally express them. This may be something that makes you uneasy at first. But, trust me, it gets easier with time and practice. Once they are known to others, then we can hold them accountable for interacting with us according to the standards we have set for ourselves.

I have set an emotional boundary for myself: I will not feel alone in my relationship. I have a desire to feel close, safe, and secure. On the flip side of that, I am willing to deliver that same expectation.

Why is that? I grew up in a household where both parents lacked healthy communication. They were present, but were not emotionally available to each other. I followed that same pattern. I was not available emotionally available in my relationships. I disconnected. I did not use my words to properly communicate my feelings, concerns or expectations.

When put in these similar scenarios, I find myself at a battle between Pre-boundary Fantajia and Fantajia 2.0.

Pre-boundary Fantajia would have smiled her way through the situations, saying nothing. She would have pretended that she was okay. She would have betrayed herself—and played herself.

Thankfully, Fantajia 2.0 is now in control. Her feelings and needs will not go neglected to make anyone else feel comfortable. Speak up, Sis!

Speak up!

In case you missed it, let's do a quick recap of boundaries that are meant for your lips to say, and for others to hear with their ears.

1. Know yourself enough to understand what you will and won't accept
2. Set those boundaries
3. If boundaries are crossed, speak up; have a conversation discussing where the line was crossed

1. Ensure everyone's on the same page going forward

Every conversation may not be smooth, and that is ok. You are beginning to speak up. You are evolving. Ideally, this should be how it plays out. You have a mature conversation. You hear each other out, and respect each other's position. A mutual agreement is reached. You will feel good. Take one "o" out of Good, you get GOD. You will feel at your highest state of being. This is a game-changer for you.

There is always a risk that it won't work out that way. People will buck. They'll have an attitude. They'll do what they need to do for them. Your job is to do what you need to do for *you*.

Setting your boundaries, staying true to them, and speaking up when someone violates them may cost you some people. Just keep in mind that your self-respect and the peace that comes from emotionally protecting yourself is worth far more.

A NO-NONSENSE GUIDE TO HANDLING SOMEONE WHO CROSSES YOUR LINE

WHAT WAS JUST SHARED with you is a great example of one of the most important things to remember about boundaries: the people you interact with need to know when they've broken yours.

Your boundaries are a line. It cannot, and should not be constantly crossed. If you consistently allow that to happen, you will feel compromised, small, and out of control of your life. Trust me, sis, that is not a good thing. Let's move correctly.

The reason why some women struggle with expressing their boundaries is it's uncomfortable to have these conversations. It's tempting to keep our boundaries invisible and never talk about them, but then be angry or disappointed when someone crosses the line.

So, we stay quiet. We allow people to push and push, and then when we can't take it anymore, or someone catches us on the wrong day, we go off like an atomic bomb. To the person on the receiving end of our rage, it seems as if we exploded out of nowhere, when in reality, our temperature had been steadily rising each time our line was crossed.

I've had to learn that you can't let your feelings bottle up until you blow up. When your boundaries are involved, speaking up is a must. If you feel something, you have to say something. Address how you feel. Consistently, and as quickly as possible. Playing in that gray area of not saying anything is easy, but it's also immature and a guaranteed recipe for disaster. You are always the one who ends up hurt and angry. When lines are crossed, be confident and mature enough to let the offender know.

With strangers, boundaries are one-time statements. With people that you care about and who you maintain a relationship with, boundaries are conversations.

In either case, communicating your stance is necessary.

To help you build your confidence in this area, here are some tips that can help you when you have to confront someone that crosses your boundary line.

Keep your calm in check. When you are hurt and angry, you may be tempted to pounce on the person, but popping off is not what we do. Women are in control. Women can remain calm. Take a moment to check your emotions, get yourself together, and then address the situation. This isn't weakness—it's maturity.

Keep it consistent. Once you set your boundary, stick to it. You cannot allow someone else to lower your standards. The boundary is the boundary. If it's broken have a conversation that explains your position and feelings. You can choose to keep that person in your circle. However, they need to respect your standards.

Get to it. Address things quickly. The passive-aggressive thing will not work. Avoiding will not work. You should never avoid confronting someone who has violated a boundary. As soon as it comes up, collect yourself and get to talking. Address it honestly. Address it early. Be upfront about what happened and how you feel about it.

Give it a little bit of time. When your boundaries are clear, you don't have to run them down whenever you meet someone. Communicating your expectations from that space indicates a lack of power. You don't have to whip out your list of rules on a first date or your first day in the office on a new job either. Rules run people, especially men, away. Standards and boundaries make people rise. Let people into your world first. Let them get to know you; and you know them. In time, as conversations become more frequent you will have an opportunity to share your boundaries. Believe me.

Use your words. Your words are your most powerful weapon. Your voice has to be heard. If your boundary is broken, speaking on it may sound like:

"Please don't _____ (You fill in the blank with your boundary)."
For example:

- "Please don't speak to me that way."
- "Please don't call me outside of my name."
- "Please don't come into my office with problems. What solutions are you considering? Let's talk through those."
- "Please don't call me when I am at work; or before 10am; or after 10pm."

You've got the words. Use them.

Hold people accountable. Communicating your boundaries gives people an opportunity to correct themselves. If someone crosses your line once, it was a mistake. If they do it again, after you've expressed how you feel about it, it's intentional. It was a decision. And you have a choice to make on the other end of that decision.

People won't know what your boundaries are. People eff up. My guy didn't intend to hurt me when he came to my house with dinner, but he did. His true intentions and the nature of our relationship made me want to have a conversation with him about my boundaries so he could understand his mistake. Now that he understands what I need, he's made the effort to respect my boundaries better. This is why communication is key.

Put your needs first. Staying true to your boundaries is not easy work, but it's essential work. You have to do this for you. Hold people accountable, as well as yourself. Don't compromise yourself. Don't be held hostage to fear of losing anything or anyone by sacrificing your self-respect. For once, put yourself first.

BEFORE YOU GO...

I want to leave you with this reminder—this is constant work.

You have a new awareness. You've determined you want to move differently. You've determined you will move differently. This is on-the-job training, ladies. This is a journey of constant learning, constant rising, and constant correction. Give your boundaries, and yourself, room to grow.

There are levels to this life. As you move through life and relationships, at every level, the same boundaries will be tested with new people. Just when you think you have it all down and your boundary boxes have been checked, you'll be in a new situation, start a new position, meet a new person, become a new person, and you'll have to revisit those same boundaries again.

Boundaries shift and change. Let them.

You'll know what you need to do for you.

BLESSINGS

"I have too many blessings to be ungrateful." Anonymous

BLESSINGS BELONG TO YOU

*I*t would be impossible for us to have a conversation about womanhood without talking about faith. As a woman moving in and through this world, you must understand the essence of who you are.

Your womanhood is rooted in your spirituality. Spirituality carries you. Spirituality covers you. Spirituality gives you peace and power. Spirituality grants you grace. Spirituality guides you. Spirituality surrounds you when you are strong and when you are weak.

Spirituality is who you are.

This is not about a specific religion. You may be Christian, Buddhist, or Muslim. It doesn't matter what you call Him. The Divine. Spirit. Source energy. Higher Power. Whatever you choose to call the God that you belong to is up to you. What matters most is that you know that you belong to someone bigger than you. What matters is that you know that you are not in this world without a God watching over you. What matters is that you know that blessings belong to you.

You just need to be bold enough to believe and receive.

Spirituality is confidence. There is nothing more feminine and powerful than a woman who is deeply connected to God. She has an assurance about her and a light around her. She doesn't allow defeat to live long. She attracts people, and only tolerates positivity. She moves with, and on purpose.

When you have a deep connection to God, you move differently. You should be led by a divine voice—an intuition—that you can always trust. You should be bolder. You should pray with power and expectation. But that expectation piece has been tripping us up, and by our own doing and lack of knowing, kept us out of the divine favor that is available to us.

It's like this: think about a baby or a young child. She looks to her mother for everything. For food when she is hungry. For a Band-aid when she is hurt. For comfort when she cries. For cupcakes, balloons, and gifts on her birthday, and toys on Christmas morning. She trusts that she will be protected and provided for by the woman who gave her life. That baby girl asks—and she expects to receive. She knows who she belongs to.

Our relationship with God is exactly the same. So, I have a question for you:

Do you know who you belong to?

I ask you this because it's so easy for us to forget that God's got us. We get used to being beaten down, broken, struggling, stressed, and living hard, heavy lives We feel forgotten; abandoned; orphaned.

As women, we're taught that life is hard. We're taught that it's a man's world. We're told that as Black girls and women, we can't dream. We have life to worry about, work to do, kids to raise. We're told that men ain't shit; that they're dogs. We've been hearing these things all our lives.

These stories are supposed to make us strong, but really these narratives have hurt us. They've hardened us. They've baked disbelief into our DNA, into our subconscious mind, into our womanhood. We've let life beat our belief down. We don't feel loved. We don't feel protected.

We need to shift that mindset.

We are loved. We are protected. We can surrender and move through life in our feminine flow and power. We can be delicate and divine. We can be vulnerable.

We can ask. We can receive. We can dream and desire more. We can love. We can surround ourselves with beauty and bounty. We can live this ridiculously abundant, happy, rich-in-every-way life.

We can do all of this because we have God.

You have been moving with constraint, restriction, and fear. You've been unwilling to allow yourself to be cared for, and held down. There are parts of you that don't believe that you deserve anything beyond the basics. But God has so much more for you. God is holding you. He is moving you. He is here.

When you look at your life, even with all its challenges, it's clear that God has been there.

There is no other explanation for what you have or the magnitude of what you've achieved and received. God has been there. You may not have asked Him for what you have, but someone has. The women before you—whether it's a great-grandmother, grandmother, a mother, an auntie—who has prayed for and over you. The energy and the faith of some woman, somewhere, past or present, is evident in your life. That's how powerful they were, and are. That's how powerful you are.

And that is how powerful and protective God is over you.

I need you to understand who you are. You are a kept woman—kept by God.

If you've forgotten that, let me remind you today. There is power in that understanding. There is power in that knowing. Ladies, great blessings are awaiting you. Miraculous things. Divine things. Big things.

Let's go get them.

In this section, we are going to get into some spiritual womanly things. We'll talk about energy, vibration, visualization, manifestation, and alignment. You may have heard these terms, tools, techniques before, or maybe this will be your first time. I am offering you recommendations from my own spiritual tool kit, and time-tested practices that women of power and faith have been using to call blessings forth long before we were born. Now, I want you to put them all to work in your life. As a woman, these are all practices you must master.

As you are reading, and hopefully, thinking about God and your relationship with Him, I want you to get planted in your spirit that everything we cover in the pages that follow comes down to one thing —trust.

Trust that you are connected to something bigger than yourself. Trust that you have an inner power. Trust that you can see something that you want, you can speak it into existence. Trust that you can talk and walk as if it already is.

Trust that God is holding you down—fully and completely.

LET GOD HOLD YOU UP WHEN YOU CAN'T

THROUGHOUT THIS BOOK, I'll be talking to you about asking God for what you want and need.

But the beauty of God is that He also shows up in moments before we can even ask. Moments when we need miracles. Moments when we need peace and His presence. In those moments, God's presence is undeniable because there is no other way to explain situations that turned around. Those moments are supernatural experiences when we're reminded of who God is, and who we are. We are His, fully and completely. We are carried and covered.

The days leading up to my mother's death felt like one connected God moment. I can still feel the energy, years later. It started on New Year's Eve of 2017. I'd dropped my daughter, Skylar-who was an infant at the time-at my mother's house, and gone to church. I'd been to services at this particular church a few times, but I didn't know anyone. Miraculously, there were seats still available near the front. I grabbed one. The service was vibrant. We praised. We worshipped. God was in the atmosphere.

At the end of the service, the pastor came down from the pulpit, and began shaking hands with those of us who sat in the first few pews. One by one, she graciously thanked each person for coming. I knew I needed to get home to get my baby, but I sat still.

"God bless you," she says, over and over again to every person. And then she gets to me.

She grabs my hand and pulls me close.

"You are full of abundance," she whispers in my ear. "Your life is about to change in a major way. You've got to get ready. Get ready right now, and God is going to be there with you to guide your steps."

With a quick hug, she moves on to the next person, as if we were strangers.

I sat in my seat, stunned. No words. A girl sitting beside me must have noticed the confusion and the clear, "what-in-the-hell-just-happened", look all over my face.

"She's a prophet," the girl told me. "She just spoke over your life."

At the time, I had no idea what prophesying was. I didn't know what to think about what I'd just heard or experienced. I thought, *"How could a woman that I'd never seen before in my life know anything about me?"* I didn't know what to do with what she told me, or if I was supposed to do anything at all. I got my purse and jacket and left.

When I got back to my mother's house, all of her grandchildren were there. She was exactly where she wanted to be. We talked for a few minutes as I packed up my daughter's things. As I began to walk out of the door, my mom said, "Give me a kiss," as she handed my daughter to me.

I cringed. She loved to kiss us on the lips; I hated it. She said goodbye to Skyler, but there was something about the way she said it that felt odd to me. God was already speaking to me.

She asked me for a kiss again, and I gave in, knowing that it meant everything to her. A kiss on her lips was so small, but it was so significant to her. I felt the instinct, the pull, to give her what she wanted.

The next day, New Year's Day, was a normal day. I got up. Took a bath. Got dressed and went to the mall. My mother had a tradition of making these delicious egg rolls, so I decided at the last minute to make a batch for her and my father for lunch. I'd just moved into my new place. It was a small apartment, but it was clean, peaceful, and most importantly, it was Skyler's and mine. I was so proud. My baby is crawling on the floor near me. My music is going. I am in good spirits. My mood is light. I am good. My daughter is good. It's the holidays. Everything is right.

The phone rang. It was my cousin. I rolled my eyes, expecting that she was calling me with some more of family drama that I wasn't in the mood for.

My spirit said, "Answer the phone." So, I did.

"Hey cousin, what's going on?"

"Yo, did your dad call you?"

"No."

"Yeah, you might want to call your dad right now. Your mom is in the hospital."

I heard what she said, but I didn't process it. "Girl, what are you talking about? I just saw my mom and nothing was wrong with her."

"No, it's serious, Fantajia."

Serious? How could that be? I was just talking to my mom. I'd just been standing in her house. I'd just kissed her on the lips a few hours before.

My body wanted to panic, but something wouldn't let me. Something came over me. I felt this intense calm-like energy, like a bolt of lightning, surging from my head to my feet. I was frozen in time, but my mind was racing. And so was my body. Peace came over me. And then instruction. Finish the food. Pack the baby's stuff. You have to go. Spirit spoke and I listened.

I picked up the phone and called my daughter's other grandmother. As soon as she answered, I don't know what made me say what came out of my mouth next.

"Hey, Le'. I need you to come and meet me at the hospital. Here is the address." I gave her a few seconds to write it down.

"I think my mom is dead." I said.

"Wait, what?" I heard her say. I could hear the shock in her voice. And confusion. I guess she was wondering how I could possibly be so calm and matter of fact when my mother had died.

I didn't know if my mom was dead. I grabbed my baby and headed to the hospital to find out. On the way there, I spoke with my family who told me that she was in the ICU. When I got to the hospital, the front desk wouldn't allow me to go up to her with my baby. As soon as her grandmother got there, I handed her over. Calmly, I got on the elevator.

Other than God's presence, there is no other way to explain the peace that came over me. When I walked into my mother's hospital room, she was so still. I knew she was gone. The machines were still going to keep her alive. There was no one there but the two of us.

I left the room and go out into the hallway. I didn't know if I was breathing or not. I found a nurse. I grab her hand, and pull her to the side. She's surprised, but she stays calm.

"Ma'am," I plead with her, with my voice and my eyes. I hold her hand tighter. "I need for you to tell me what's real because I have to protect myself right now. Let me know what's happening."

"I am not supposed to tell you that." That was the truth. I knew that doctors usually delivered that type of news to families; I was asking her to break rules for me. But I needed to know.

"Please."

"Your mom is not going to make it. I'm so sorry."

Since I was the only one there before the family can come, I was able to sit in silence with her and prepare myself.

The only person I needed at that moment was my Aunt Cyn. God told me to call her. And if there was ever a moment that I needed her and God, it was that one. I dialed her number.

"Hey, Auntie. It's me," I spoke calmly. "My mom is in the hospital and the family is on their way down here. I need you to come and cover me through this."

How did I know I needed that? I can't tell you. But I knew I did.

In what felt like minutes, Auntie was there in the room with me. I sat quietly by the bed, holding my mom's hand for the last time. I was at peace with my Mommy. When it got hard, my auntie was there to stand in faith with me.

As soon as she took her last machine breath, everything around me started to come into order. My family filtered out, and once again, I was alone. Moving in the Spirit, I completed the paperwork for my mother's death certificate. I went home. I got up the next day, called her job, and let them walk me through filing the claim for her life insurance. I went to the bank, withdrew enough from her account to pay my dad's rent on their place for two months. Her taxes and final bills were handled. Within a week, I'd put her to rest.

My daughter was the only one who really watched me grieve. To the world, I was normal. I went back to work the week after the funeral. But getting through the day took all the strength I had. For weeks, I did nothing. Almost like Skyler was caring for herself. I would make her bottles and have them out, change her Pampers (trademark name that should always be capitalized), and little baby would let mommy rest.

Some family criticized me, questioning if I even loved my mom since I didn't publicly fall apart. Hell, my sister said I pulled the plug, all kinds of craziness.

I was changing. I lost my mom, but I knew that there was no need for tears. I gained an angel who I call on all the time to move on my behalf.

I gained a new force. The only way to honor her memory and to celebrate her was to live out loud. My mother's experience spiritually shifted me.

Like the pastor who prophesied over my life, God was guiding my steps. He guided me through my mother's death and my grief. I'd always known God, but that was the moment that I began to know Him deeply and differently than I ever had before. I knew what it felt like to be carried through something that could have destroyed me. I was supported in the Spirit. Loved. Cared for. Protected.

I was held up in a way that I, nor anyone else but God, could have.

When and where has God held you? What times in your life should you have completely fallen apart, but there was a spirit that held you and protected you from the chaos that tried to come for you?

It took me a few years to process the magnitude of what God did for me. And then I started to replay other moments in my life where He'd been there, time and time again.

Maybe you haven't lost a parent yet, but you lost someone else you loved deeply. Maybe you felt like you have even lost yourself. Maybe you've lived through some other type of pain that should have crushed you emotionally. Or maybe your heart hasn't been broken yet. But know that in those moments, when they come, you will be full of peace from now on when you understand the concept, "Let God hold you up when you can't".

I know it is hard when, in the middle of situations, people tell us, "Let go and let God", "It is a reason for every season." Look, let's keep it real, no one wants to hear that when they are going through stuff!

Let me let you in on a little secret, When life gets too hard, and you are attempting to operate from a place of peace, you have to be completely unbothered by the reality. How do you do this? Live in the spirit; live in believe mode.

We'll dig deeper into walking in God's power to break through tough times.

The way we do this? We speak a word. Whenever chaos, big or small, tries to come for you, speak a word of peace over that moment.

Say to yourself, "I am at peace." "I am in control." And, so it is.

You'll completely shift the moment. You'll make way for God to do His thing—which is to hold you up and hold you down.

When you move in this sort of certainty, people, will call you cold. They will call you crazy. They won't understand the God in you. But they don't need to. Your only job is to show up. The game is to be sold, not told.

GOD IS BIGGER THAN YOUR BELIEF

et's be real. Some of us have inherited spirituality from someone else. We only in it because our parents were in it. We inherit and adopt but we do not properly study what we say we believe. In fact, many times we just accept the information we have been fed. For myself, I became aware of the power of belief while in college. I attended a private Christian college, where I was privileged to study multiple belief systems. So, I am speaking from some experience. I've learned that all religions have structure and that the base foundation is love. God is Love.

In my household, we practice Christianity. It is important for me to teach my family not to just recite words, but to live the word.

Growing up, I had a surface level understanding of God. I learned scriptures, but was not taught to apply them. We prayed weak prayers. We barely believed that God could do all things—at least not for us in my household.

You may be moving through life, living in lack, believing that is the kind of life that you are destined for. This is especially true with money. Church and culture can portray wealth as something that is reserved for a chosen few, dangling it like a carrot in front of the eyes of everyday people. Struggle is celebrated and praised, as if it is the ultimate sacrifice.

But if we really knew and believed God's word, we'd know that being poor is a sin. God wants you to be rich because He wants you to be wise, at ease, wealthy, beautiful women. A poor person is an ignorant person. That is not what God wants or has for you. Forget what you've heard.

The Bible is the realest book on prosperity. God talks directly to us about wisdom and money and how we should desire and cultivate wealth.

Look at these scriptures to see what God really wants for you (these are only a few):

"FOR I KNOW the thoughts that I think towards you, saith the Lord, thoughts of peace and not of evil to give you the expected end." Jeremiah 29:11

"Build ye houses, and dwell in them; and plant gardens, and eat the fruit of them." Jeremiah 29: 6"The Lord your God will make you abound in all the work of your hands, in the fruit of your body, in the increase of your livestock, and the produce of your land for good. For the lord will again rejoice over you for good as He rejoices over your fathers." Deuteronomy 30:9

"The blessing of the Lord, it maketh rich, and he addeth no sorrow with it." Proverbs 10:22

"God is in the midst of: she shall not be moved; God will help her when morning dawns." Psalm 46:5

"The wisest of women builds her house, but folly with her own hands tears it down." Proverbs 14:1

"Do not let your adorning be external; the braiding of the hair and the putting on of gold jewelry, or clothing you wear; but let your adorning be the hidden person of the heart with the imperishable beauty of a gentle and quiet spirit, which in God's sight is very precious." 1 Peter 3:3-4

"She opens her mouth with wisdom and the teaching of kindness is on her tongue." Proverbs 31:26

"You are altogether beautiful. my love; there is no flaw in you." Song of Solomon 4: 7

IT'S time to amplify your beliefs. God clearly has more for you. It doesn't have to be only about money in the bank. We're talking about every area of your life. Your career. Your home. Your children. Your business. Your purpose. You can ask God for the big things. Whatever it is that you have put limits on, take them off. Take that tiny little box that you've put your belief in, dust it off, and go bigger.

You aren't begging God to meet your needs anymore. You have wants. You have desires and dreams.

Believe God for *all of it*.

Believe God to take you from paycheck to pure abundance.

Believe God to take you from dating just any man to a purpose partner.

Believe God to take you from just a job to a career that feeds you financially and fulfills your purpose.

Once you shift your mind to believe bigger, God will go bigger for you.

YOU HAVE TO SEE IT TO BELIEVE IT

IT IS one thing to want something—it's another thing to go get it.

As you read through this section, you will notice that I am bold when it comes to believing, prayer, and faith. I believe that we have a grace on our lives and a God-given power that can give us whatever we want. You have dreams, desires, and plans that God has planted in you. You are here to become the highest, biggest version of the woman God created you to be. There is nothing that you want, big or small, that God will deny you as you become her.

But first, you need to see it. You need to get clear on what you desire.

71

You need a vision.

I know you've heard some variation of the words, "Write it down and make it plain" Those words are directly from scripture, specifically Habakkuk 2:2, in which God instructs Habakkuk to write the vision (or in some versions of the Bible, the word "vision" is translated as "revelation"). In that same scripture, God directs Habakkuk to not just write the vision on tablets, but write it clearly so that whoever reads it can run with it. The word that we get from God is to *write it* and go *do* something. We'll get to that go-do part in a few pages, but for now, let's focus on downloading this vision that we need to write.

Vision is the grand plans that God has for you. He knows what those plans are, and now it's time for you to know them too. You need to know how to move intentionally through this life—be clear about where you are going and why. This is why understanding your vision is necessary. Vision gives you the clarity and purpose that every woman needs.

So, what does vision look like? Let's talk about that.

Here are the hallmarks of vision:

Vision expands. Your vision is not small. When you ask, God may give you an entire vision, or He may only give you a glimpse of the vision. (Does not make sense here) You are here to be fruitful and multiply. There is so much for you to do. As you move, gain more wisdom, and prepare, there will be another level. There will be higher heights. There will be bigger ideas, dreams, and desires. These are signs that your vision is expanding. Grow into it.

Vision is bigger than you. Your vision serves you and other people. Those people could be your family, your children, or your community. God created you to influence and impact other people. Whatever you dream about, I am sure you've thought about the people that are coming with you. You want something bigger so that you can do more for someone else. Your higher purpose is always attached to people.

Vision can't be completed without God. Your vision is God-given. So, God will provide. He will do what you can't do. He will bring people and resources. He will open doors to opportunities.

Everyone and everything you need has to come through God. So, if you think it's all on you—it's not. God's got this and He's got you.

As you begin to think about the vision God has for you, I want you to start with a prayer to unlock your heart and spirit and unleash your clarity.

Here is a prayer that I pray when I need God to make my vision clear:

Father God, give me the ability to see. Give me a glimpse of what that big picture for my life looks like so that I know how to move accordingly. Give me the foresight. Give me the vision. Give me goals. Bring the people who are going to help me to bring it all into fruition.

Next, allow God to download into you. Get a notebook, and start writing what comes to you when you ask yourself these four big questions:

- Who am I?
- Why am I here?
- Who do I want to be?
- What is the highest and biggest vision that I have for my life?

How does that feel to you? Are you feeling good? Are you feeling free? I want you to begin to open your heart, mind, and spirit up to purpose and possibility again. I want you to start seeing who you can be, and what you can have. Anything. Everything. What you wrote out is not some far-fetched fairytale. It isn't a figment of your imagination. These are real dreams. Tangible dreams. A life that will live and have. This is your promise. This is your vision. This is something that has worked for me.

And once you have a crystal-clear vision, it's stamped by God. It's yours. It is safe for you to believe your vision, to fall in love with it, because you can have it. *You will have it.*

Get excited. See it. Feel it. Believe it.

Now, we have to work.

ACTIVATING THE VISION

our vision is only as good as the work that you put in to bring it to fruition. Yes, God gave you an assignment. But He won't give you the action. He won't do the work for you. You have to bring the blessing to you.

Whenever I need to get into alignment with my vision and go get what's mine, I work the same eight-step system to activate my faith and flow:

1. Pray.
2. Write it down.
3. Visualize it.
4. Ask God for wisdom.
5. Believe it's already done.
6. Work the plan.
7. Receive the blessing.
8. Rinse and repeat.

LET me break down each of these steps for you.

Step 1: Pray.

We are women who don't make moves without prayer. You want to pray to get on the same page with God. To confirm His partnership with what you want, and to prepare yourself for the work ahead.

Prayer isn't complicated. It is you and God in conversation. It is you speaking and requesting, and Him confirming. Submit your request to God. Get into agreement with Him.

When you've prayed and your spirit is at peace, then God has confirmed your ask. You are filled up with the faith to move.

Step 2: Write it down.

We talked about this in the previous section, but writing out your vision is so important. Writing out your vision is like creating your map to your destined destination. You need something to keep you on your path, to guide you to where you are going, and redirect you if you get lost.

Get into a quiet, prayer-filled, and peaceful place. Write out the vision. You may want to write out your vision in words or you may want to create a vision board with pictures and images of what your vision looks like. You can do both. You choose. The point is that you need something tangible that you can see.

I love putting my vision and prayers on paper. I have notebooks filled with dreams.

When I was making $32,000 a year, I wrote down that I wanted $56,000. When God gave me that, I wanted to elevate again to $80,000 a year to live a better life. God has given me that—and then some. As I elevated to each of those levels, I could go back to what I'd written to remind myself of where God was moving me to.

Putting your vision on paper is powerful. Do it.

Step 3: Visualize it.

This is where you want to make your vision real. You've prayed. You've written the vision. Do you sit there and stare at it? No. You get up.

Put yourself in the atmosphere and environment of what you want so you can feel the energy of the vision and expectation.

If you want a BMW, go to the BMW dealership. Sit in the car. See how the leather feels. See how the wheel feels in your hands. Inhale the scent of the interior and let it fill your nose. Imagine yourself on the freeway, music blaring, breeze blowing. Feel all of it.

You can do this with a model home, the building that you want to own, the corporate offices of the company where you want to work.

Get into the space of your vision so it can get real. When it happens, you'll already know how it feels.

Step 4: Ask God for wisdom.

God is your partner and constant guide. He has resources and people lined up to support your vision. He has the steps you need to take and the moves you need to make. Ask Him.

This is a prayer that I use when I need God to help me move:

Father God, equip me with the tools and the people that I need to be in position to do your work. What do you want from me, God? How can I help you, God? Put me in position for you. Father God, put your goals to work. Who am I here to serve? Bring those people forth.

Always go to God for direction and protection.

Step 5: Believe it's already done.

I can't stress this enough. When you want something; when you and God have decided that it already is, everything in your being *has to* believe that it is already done. Don't slip or sleep on this. You are a woman—and not just any woman. You are a powerful woman. A provided for woman. A protected one. A woman who is the daughter of a King. You move with the supreme confidence that anything you want is yours. You start to move with force, with expectation, when you understand that there is a force behind you. You shouldn't be shocked when you receive anything. You are blessed.

Step 6: Work the plan.

Visions become goals. Goals become work. Your actions must match your task. Do the legwork and put yourself in position to receive what God is preparing for you.

If you want wealth in the form of money, do you have the wisdom, the financial planning skills, the accountant, that you need? You can't manage millions if you can't manage a dollar.

I want to speak on big stages and platforms. That means I have to set goals to grow my speaking ability.

I have to practice speaking techniques, like enunciating properly and strengthening the muscles in my jaw so I am clear to audiences.

This is what the goals and the work look like. Goals are where I want to go, and the work is the action that it takes to get there.

It could be the dancer in me, but I know that miracles happen in movement. You have to move.

Step 7: Receive the blessing.

Blessings are the fruit of prayer. You are simply receiving what you've asked for. This is grace. This God. You don't have to do anything but receive.

When your vision becomes your reality, give gratitude. As your blessings begin to flow, give praise. Cross that thing off your list. Tell somebody. Buy yourself something. Celebrate yourself!

Step 8: Rinse and repeat.

Set a new goal. Move on to the next. You are in a season of purpose, and you don't have time to let grass grow under your feet. Pray about the next level of your vision, write it, see it, and work it.

ACCELERATING YOUR BLESSINGS

*T*his spirituality thing is fluid. And it's personal. So, you get to decide how you and God are going to move. And I wouldn't be a good teacher and mentor if I didn't give you shortcuts and cheat codes.

As you move through the eight steps that we walked through to activate your faith, I suggest working and repeating it until you master it. Once you can flow through those steps with ease, this abbreviated version is equally as powerfully to put your vision in motion and to start manifesting blessings:

Pray. This never changes. You need God's ear, energy, and connection. Speak your requests. Get God's confirmation. Come back to check in as you move.

Write it out. You still need to see it. Get your notebook or journal and write out the vision and the goals. Pull out magazines and make your vision board.

Hold the vision. When I am in manifestation mode, I hold the vision every day. I do this through prayer, meditation, and movement.

I am constantly talking to God. In meditation, I am taking time to get still; to center myself and connect with God. For my movement, I am doing what feels right to me and when I feel guided by God. I am constantly coming back to the vision and doing the work. I touch the things that I want in some way so that I can feel them until I have them. These are actions that align with my task and keep me in the energy of what I am waiting for.

Stay in the space of the vision.

Receive the blessing. What you want is what God wants for you. As soon as you ask, God will begin to bend and conform everything around you to bring that blessing to you. Expect your request to be expedited. Expect that your blessing to arrive at any moment.

When I decided to write this book, I knew it would be a huge expense.

I decided that it was happening and I started the work that I knew I needed to do. I prayed for it. I wrote it out. I connected with the team to help me bring the project together and started paying them knowing that I would have the funds to continue those payments until the end. Within weeks, new orders for my jewelry came in. I hadn't advertised or promoted anything. I didn't have to. God knew what I wanted and why. The "how" was not my responsibility—it was His.

My prayers are a peek into my current world. When I need a laptop or a surge of money to meet my current needs or fulfill a level of the vision, I am asking God specifically for those things. Everything I need is connected to His purpose for me. It's all a part of the bigger picture. The same is true for you.

As what you pray for starts to flow to you, know it when you see it. God will suddenly increase the sales in your business. He'll send that person who owes you money from years ago with repayment in hand. He'll put you in the room with somebody who knows some-body at the company you want to interview for.

Your blessings can show up in many forms. Recognize and receive them when they do.

PRAY POWERFULLY

I was probably in my late twenties before I really understood what prayer was. Prayer is how we communicate with God; it's simply conversation. We are so focused on getting prayer wrong, when that is impossible to do. Just talk to Him.

Prayer is part of our daily lives and anytime you pray, it should reflect the power you have and the God you serve. When you request anything from God, this is how you do it:

Know who you are.

You are a daughter to a King.

During his presidency, do you think Barack Obama's daughters moved through The White House with a whisper, asking for permission to have this or have that? No. They knew that they were in their father's house. As you move through the earth, you too are in your Father's house. Walk in your power.

You have the Holy Spirit behind you. God has prepared and protected you. Don't pray from a weak or meek place.

Fill your prayers up. God is not a little God. Stop asking for the small in life. Instead of asking for a job, ask God for the next level in your life where you are earning that $75,000 (or whatever a big salary looks like for you right now). Instead of asking God for the $100 that you need for your electric bill, ask Him for overflow and permanent financial peace.

I know that, sometimes, you need a miracle moment. You need God to handle a money situation and cover you for the month. That is okay at times. But I don't want "just enough" to be a lifestyle for you.

When it comes to money, try something like this:

God, I need you to give me the vision to monetize my gifts and make this money every month without having to clock in for somebody.

Don't go to God begging for small things. Ask above the need. Ask for the big vision.

You don't have to settle for the scraps when you can have the supernatural; the above-and-beyond blessings. That is not only what you deserve, but this is what *your* God has the capacity to provide.

Speak bigger. When we bring our problems to our homegirls, we come with all the base in our voice and, "Girl-can-you-believe-he-did-and-she-said," swag that we have. We're wide open with our problems and pain. But when we go to God, we come hesitantly, properly, with our voices barely above a whisper. God wants your reverence, but He also wants your realness. Don't play shy and meek with him. Go boldly. Speak loudly. Be comfortable. Be a woman. Be human. Be His.

Expect it.

If you are interviewing for a job, and you've asked God for the position, become the woman who has that position. Go to the mall and buy that $75 blouse so you feel like wearing to the interview. Feel that fabric on your skin so you move differently. Step into the power.

Speak like you have the position.

Walk in like you deserve it—because you do.

Walk out like you have it—because you do.

The expectation is the manifestation that what you've requested, what you've prayed for, will happen. Put yourself in alignment with that. You are creating the vibration, the energy, of expectation.

Move. Do the legwork. Put yourself in position to receive. Once you and God decide it's happening, you have to prepare. Move in the direction of what you want.

If you want a new home, how are you financially preparing and saving for it? Have you priced the neighborhood? Cleaned up your credit? Applied for mortgages?

If you want to start a business, have you filed for your LLC? Opened the business bank account? Opened your mouth to tell people what you sell?

Wanting and waiting is not enough. You must move.

Keep in touch. Always remember that prayer is constant communication with God. Use prayer to connect with God as you move throughout your day. When you are praying for something specific, don't put your prayers down until you see the fruit in the form of the blessings.

BECOMING

"*The woman you are becoming will cost you people, relationships, spaces and material things.*
Choose her over everything." *Author Unknown*

THE JOURNEY OF BECOMING

I hope that, by now, you are beginning to feel differently.

The words that you've read, the shifts that you've made, the vision that you now have for your life, the power that you know realize that you have, the God that is in your corner...SIS! All of this is happening to, for, and within you.

You are stepping into unmarked territory. This is a new chapter in your book. A new level of your spirituality. A new level of your womanhood. You are a new woman.

A woman who has new standards—and she is setting them.

A woman who is creating the boundaries she needs—and she is expressing them.

A woman who knows how she needs God to move in her life—and she's telling Him.

A woman who is beginning to tap into her spiritual and feminine flow.

Your mind is expanding. Your heart is expanding. Your hand is expanding, to hold everything that life has to offer you.

You are a sacred woman, a new woman, a new being. This is the woman you are becoming.

Becoming the evolving into the highest, most supreme, godliest version of yourself. Becoming is moving in your full power of faith and love. Becoming is being, doing, and having whatever you want. Becoming is a personal process.

Whenever I think about becoming, the image that always comes to mind is a caterpillar that is transitioning to a butterfly. At some point in our lives, probably in an elementary-school science class, we learned that the beautiful, bright butterfly didn't start her life as what we see today. Butterflies begin as a furry caterpillar on the ground. Our teachers make this process sound very light and easy, almost romantic. But there is a lot of mess that goes down in that cocoon the caterpillar creates for itself before a beautiful butterfly can emerge.

The process is called metamorphosis. I'll spare you all the nasty details, but what is important to know is that the caterpillar goes through some hard things in this transformation process.

To become a butterfly, the caterpillar must fall completely apart. Each piece of the caterpillar unravels and becomes undone until it becomes a liquid version of itself. And from that liquid, the butterfly begins to build itself from scratch. Intricately and intentionally.

The butterfly's body changes. What it eats changes. How it moves changes. In the end, the caterpillars unrecognizable.

The becoming process isn't easy—but what emerges is so beautiful.

I tell you that to prepare you, not scare you.

This process of becoming the woman you want to be comes down to these five key things:

- **Shit gets real.** This process is hard. There will be pressure, sacrifice, and being really uncomfortable at times. But the result that is waiting for you on the other side of your metamorphosis is worth every bit of the sacrifice and shedding that you will have to go through.

- **It's personal.** If you notice, not every butterfly looks the same. There are different species and colors. There are more than 17,000 types of butterflies in the world. Each one of them is special; each one of them is beautiful in their own, unique way. Know that your journey may not look like everyone else's. No one else may understand it at first. And that is okay. This is your process, one that isn't about perfection but constant correction. You are learning, growing, and changing.

- **Transformation happens in stages.** A caterpillar doesn't create a cocoon one night and wake up the next morning as a butterfly. It takes days—even weeks—for that process to be complete. Your transformation process may take weeks. It may take months, or a year. You will get there in time. And you will have to transform—to become—again and again. The woman you need to be in your twenties is not who you need to be in your thirties, forties, or fifties. With each age, there is a new stage. Become the woman you need to be today and be prepared to grow again when it's time.

- **Don't look back.** The caterpillar that once was is nowhere near what the butterfly is. The caterpillar will never be again. You will never be the woman you once were again, so there is no need to look back at her—mistakes and all. Becoming is about focusing forward.

- **You will be new.** You get to have new skin. You get to take flight. You get to become a new you. And you get to take everything that you are, everything that you've been through, and everything that you've learned to *become*.

When you become, you can just be. You know who you are. You know what you are worth. You know what you bring to the table. You know you have the power to manifest, to create, and to bring life into whatever you decide to touch. You know how to bring order into your life, and to move away from chaos and into certainty.

Getting into this place of knowing—of becoming—is your process. And to manage your process, you need tools. These tools will help you to continue to build your core and maneuver through the challenges that come with growth.

That is what this section of the book is about.

We'll get into the tools—mental, spiritual, and physical—to help you stay grounded in yourself as you move through this next phase of your womanhood, and the rest of your life.

Let me teach you the ways of womanhood that will allow you to get right with yourself. Let me teach you how to get so good with yourself and God that nothing will cause you to question, or forget, who you are.

Let me teach you how to *become*.

STAYING IN THE SPIRIT

We talked a lot about God and the power of prayer in the last section of the book, setting our spiritual foundation. You have the start of your spiritual house. Now let's get into holding your house up.

And that is staying in the spirit.

Faith is one of those things that you can't ever let go of. Your faith will be challenged constantly. When the wait is too long. When challenges come. When something—or someone—leaves you. Life. When you think that you finally got the thing that you've been praying for, only for it to be another job or man, meant for practice and preparation, not permanent residence in your life.

These are the times that try women's souls, and when you need to figure out how to pull yourself back into the space of knowing.

Here's what it is:

There is believing in God—and then there is *believing God*.

Believing God is knowing that He *always* comes through. There is no need to be anxious or afraid. There is no need to keep looking out of the window, waiting for the delivery person to bring the blessings box to your doorstep. He said what He said.

It's coming, sis.

What's interesting about womanhood is that we believe that as we age and mature, it means that we always have all the answers. We believe that we'll be waiting and wondering less about our lives and who we will be, that we will know exactly what is going to happen when. And there is a little bit of truth to that. As grown women, we do ask less questions.

Because we know the answer.

We can settle into a space of certainty that everything that is for me (that means you) will come eventually. When it's ready—when we're ready—whatever we desire will arrive.

That is where the faith comes in.

It can be hard to settle into the spirit, the knowing, that your prayers are being answered. As you are evolving, calling more into your life, and becoming, you will have to maintain your peace, always.

Here are some tools to help you do that:

- **Give yourself permission.**

So MANY OF us have been told "no" so much in our lives. How many times, when you were a little girl, did you go into a store and see candy or some little toy that you had to have, but your momma said no? For a while, you kept asking. But eventually, you gave up on getting anything.

- **Get rid of stuff.**

God is a God of order. I mentioned this in the last section of this book, but it's crucial enough to repeat. To stay in the spirit of expectation, there must be room in your life. I don't care if it's new shoes in the closet, a new business, a new love, a new deposit in your bank account—any answered prayer—you need somewhere to put it. Where is the space in your closet, on your calendar, or in your life for what you want? Keep it open and available for what you want. Make room.

Clean up and clean out your physical and mental space. Your energy and your environment must be ready, always.

- **Get quiet.**

When I am in the place of expectation, once I get in agreement with God, I write the vision, and I get really quiet and still. I've found this to be so important in my spiritual growth. It is amazing what can happen when we get quiet. We hear God more, so we can move when He says move.

When you get quiet and still, you will get to know that stirring in your spirit that will always lead you. That is your internal GPS. When you feel it, move. Don't neglect the hunch. There is something on the other side. If it feels right, do it. You can't go wrong.

One more thing in getting quiet: sometimes, the only voice that needs to be a constant in your ear is God's. Whenever you pick up the phone to call someone to vent, think twice about it. Whenever you feel an urge to tell just any 'ole person your dreams, think three times about that. Keep some life, some dreams, some prayers, for yourself.

- **Guard your gates.**

I guard my gates, and make sure that everything around me supports and lifts me. I'll go days without music and months without television, if need be. If I choose to listen to something, I only listen to things that put and keep me in a really high vibration. In my house, in my car, wherever I am, I surround and submerge myself in positive vibes. I am signaling to God that I am ready to shift. You should do the same. Pick your podcasts and playlists with intention. Keep yourself lifted.

- **Give it up.**

What you want will likely require sacrifice—giving up some part of yourself to have something more. It requires commitment. It requires work. You will need to learn more about yourself, your mind, and your body. That requires reading and study. Changing your relationships. Changing your diet. Changing your prayer life. All of that means giving up old ways, time, money, something. Success in any area of your life will always require some type of sacrifice.

Can you withdraw from what's in right now, what's cool right now, what everybody else is doing, what social media says is poppin'? Can you sacrifice physically and financially? Can you go through short-term pain for long-term pleasure? Can you do that?

Be willing to give up.

- **Give.**

There is a guaranteed way to feel rich, regardless of what your money looks like in the moment.

Give something to somebody else.

A few years ago, I was believing God for a big financial blessing. So, I filled my little coin purse with quarters. My guy and I were hanging out. I decided to take a quarter and deposit it into every meter I saw on the block. Each quarter equaled thirty minutes of time, and I know I saved somebody (probably a lot of people) from getting tickets that day. With expired meter tickets averaging $200 each, the value of what I gave was so much more than those quarters. I gave away $3000 that day. Something that seemed so small was actually so much more.

Giving is a part of my manifestation practice.

One week, I went downtown and bought a dozen roses and an individual sleeve for each. I drove throughout the city, and whenever I saw a woman walking, I would stop my car, get out, and hand her a rose. Every time, I'd say, "You're so beautiful!" The love I received in return from every woman I met was so beautiful. Each of them returned my compliment with such joy. It was so much fun to bless somebody else. I needed to give love to receive the love that I was asking God for.

You may not put money in meters or deliver roses to women, but you can give something. Give compliments. Give your time. Give a bigger tip to a waitress or a delivery person. Find ways to give and watch how it brings blessings back to you.

LET'S TALK ABOUT SELF-LOVE

*W*hile we are on the topic of giving, let's talk about giving yourself something valuable and precious—and that's love.

You are becoming a woman who loves herself. A woman who adores herself. A woman who looks in the mirror and sees herself. A woman who is ripping out any pages in her old story that have told her that she is anything less than what she is—beautiful, worthy, revered, and respected.

If hearing those words felt uncomfortable to you, then that is exactly why you're holding this book.

Like everything else about womanhood, self-love takes work. Accepting the perfection in our imperfection is a process. To be able to look in the mirror and see yourself, to love your beauty and your body, from head to toe, is not something that comes naturally to most women. And while self-love is not just about the physical, for many of us, it starts there.

We live in a world where our self-esteem is always under attack. We're being compared to other women. With every criticism, every rejection, our confidence gets chopped down, bit by bit.

We're constantly fighting to build ourselves up. We chase acceptance, even if it's secretly.

We live so much of our lives wanting and waiting to be chosen. It's behavior that we learned as little girls.

But we are grown now.

We are becoming women who love ourselves, deeply and completely. Because affirmation and adoration from others will come and go. But our love for ourselves has to be here to stay.

When I was pregnant with my daughter, I realized, for the first time in my life that colorism was real.

My daughter's father was a broken man. He lacked confidence. Didn't earn a dollar from a job the entire time that we were together. He was verbally abusive to me, and his words hurt as much as a slap or a punch did. He spewed all his lack, all his low self-esteem, all his brokenness, on me.

He would say things like, "Oh yeah, I can't really bring you around because you're not light-skinned. In my family, we only date light-skinned women with good hair."

He called me "Bitch" like it was my first name.

I am a beautiful, brown-skinned, curvy woman. But I wasn't beautiful to him.

And I dealt with that because there were pieces of me that were broken too.

Throughout our entire relationship and my entire pregnancy, the verbal blows kept coming, not only from him, but from his family too.

My boyfriend's other daughter, my daughter's sister, who was two years old at the time, walked up to me at a family dinner.

"Your baby is going to be dark and ugly. Just like you," she said clearly and naturally, as if she were reciting her ABCs.

These were the words and the conversations that she'd heard from the adults around her, people who my unborn daughter shared a bloodline with. People who saw my beautiful brown skin as ugly.

When that little girl said that, I not only felt that pain for myself, I felt it more for my daughter. In the womb, my baby girl was fighting against the odds. She was already fighting against rejection because she wouldn't look like the other women and girls in her family.

I knew that she would never want for anything in the material sense. I was her mother, and I wouldn't allow that to happen. I would give her the best of everything from the beginning. And as her mother, I was also her protector. I wouldn't allow her to grow up feeling unloved, unwanted, or anything less than the gift that she was. In my mind, that meant praying that she would be born perfect, so no one would ever call "ugly." I trusted that God would do that for me.

I would pray to God, "God, please make my baby beautiful and chocolate with perfect eyebrows."

When I saw her for the first time, it was like looking in the mirror. She was everything that I'd prayed for.

And she looked exactly like me.

I believe that was the first time that I accepted that I must be beautiful too. Six years ago, I gave birth to a baby girl—and my confidence. God sent her to me to allow me to see myself. She began my healing, my journey towards self-love. We were both born that day.

From the moment that she was born, I began pouring affirmations into her.

Every day, she says, "I am beautiful. I am strong."

These are the words that I know she needs to hear. I know that because these were the words that *I* needed to hear.

And so do you.

You are beautiful. You are strong. You are the good thing.

When I say "the good thing," I mean you are worthy. You are the gift and the prize. You should expect to be selected, to be chosen, to be pursued. Even with curves or a slenderness that may be considered too skinny for some. Even with brown or light skin. Even with full lips. All of it is good. God-given good.

You are the good thing—always.

Self-love is not just about looks. You are so much more than hair and skin.

Self-love is loving every part of yourself, outside and in.

Self-love is trusting yourself. Giving yourself grace to make mistakes. Honoring yourself enough to step out of environments and away from people that no longer serve you. All of those are indications that you understand your value, and that you can always be good with *you*, regardless of what anyone else thinks.

Self-love is a journey. Trust me, this is not something that you can —or will—conquer overnight. It takes time and commitment. It takes affirming yourself and coming back to those words, "You are beautiful. You are strong. You are the good thing," over and over again.

Learn to love you—all of you—so that you can recognize that kind of love when it comes your way.

LET YOUR HEART OPEN UP

*A*s women, we are love.

We give it and we receive it. We need love like we need the air we breathe. Love is a beautiful thing.

And life is hard to live without it.

Let's just get into it.

Your experiences have broken your heart. When life is hard, love becomes harder. Too hard and too risky to try. So, we close our hearts and our love off.

For me, love had to be learned. My family loved me, but I didn't really love them. I carried so much resentment, hurt, and disappointment. Emotionally, I was cut off from them.

We could share a meal together, talk on the phone, go through the motions. There was a relationship, but there was no connection, at least not for me. I thought that's what love was. I didn't know how to go deep with anyone, to really allow anyone in.

Becoming a mother changed that for me.

I decided to have my daughter because I wanted to let some love into my life. I wanted to know what unconditional love felt like. With her, I felt like I had a clean slate. I could unlearn everything that I'd ever known about relationships and love, and start over. I've retaught myself what mothering means and redefined it for our family from this point forward. Until her, I was so focused on proving to the world that I could survive. With my daughter, my heart softened. At twenty-five years old (that's how old I was when I had her) I learned what love and attachment felt like for the first time.

While I am redefining motherhood for myself, believe me, love is something I am still learning on many levels. I have relationships in my life that are still broken. As I am writing this book, it's been three years since I've seen my father. He lives ten minutes from me, and has never been to my home or spent time with his granddaughter. Like many women, I am still growing to love my family in many ways.

This journey of opening my heart up fully has become religion to me. I practice it daily. I am intentional about it. I am growing to love myself. I am growing to push past the brokenness of my past with men, and learning to let a man in. I am determined to keep loving, to keep growing to accept myself, working on myself, preparing for the life partner that I want at some point—when it's time.

Love is seed to me, so I plant it with the expectation that it will come back to me and continue to reap a harvest in my life.

Sis, it's time for you to start sowing seed.

If you want love, be it from family, friends, a partner, then you need to be love.

This is your reminder and your release of all the hurt that your heart and spirit are carrying from your past. Give yourself the permission to soften your edges. You can give love. You can be loved.

The truth is, you need people. A lesson that I've had to learn as a woman is that God shows up in the form of other people. He will deliver blessings to you through others. There are people who you need to align with to make your life bigger and better. People need to see the fruit on you and the God in you. When that happens, blessings will flow through you and to you. God created you to be a blessing to people too. You are a woman who was born to nourish and build community—it is your nature.

Don't close yourself off anymore. Open your heart to let love in.

Love will require more of you. Love requires acceptance and tolerance of yourself and others. Love requires vulnerability and transparency.

But before any of that, love requires forgiveness.

I know you've heard the words, "hurt people hurt people." Hurt people have hurt us. People like our parents and partners. And we have hurt others from our hurt.

We all make mistakes. So, we have to forgive, starting with ourselves.

Before you can forgive anybody else, you have to forgive yourself. Make peace with where you went wrong, what you did and what you said, the people you hurt. Today is the day that you stop holding yourself back from love and punishing yourself for not knowing.

There was no way you could have known.

We don't just wake up self-aware and call ourselves out on the areas that require growth. Many of us have no idea that we're carrying chaos around inside.

Think about someone who smokes cigarettes in their home. Smoke has penetrated everything in that house—their hair, their clothes, their furniture. But because they've smoked for so long, they don't even smell it anymore. For that person, there is no need for fans and Febreeze. The smell is normal.

But when someone new comes into the space, the smoke hits them in the face.

When we are filled with unforgiveness, our lives are filled with a smoke that we can't smell.

It takes someone coming into our lives who can point out the bitterness and the brokenness. Sometimes they stay with us while we heal, sometimes they don't.

But you have to step out of that stale air and see your smoke; those emotionally broken places; the shattered self-esteem, and the hurt you've been surrounded by for far too long.

For me, I didn't step out until the moment that I forgave my mom. That shifted everything for me.

I had my daughter at twenty-five years old, and once I became a mother, I saw my own mother so much differently than I ever had before.

I realized that before she was my mother, she was a woman. She moved in the world with what she had and with what she knew. She moved from a space of necessity and did what she had to do to create happiness and security for herself. I judged her for being weak when really, she was a private, shy woman who had never been given the chance to flourish. When she became a mother, she was still carrying baggage from her own childhood, and adding more as she survived through life, experiencing her own hurts and heartbreaks. She did the best she could with what she had.

As I saw her as a woman, there was nothing I could blame her for anymore. I couldn't blame her for anything, or my father. They were two young people trying to survive.

My parents' behavior and who they were as children and young adults had nothing to do with me. Yet who they were as my parents had everything to do with me. Neither of them knew how to love fully.

At some point in our lives, we've looked at other families—both real and fantasy—and, in our hearts, held our parents to those expectations. But we have to understand that our families are different. Their journeys were different, which means our journeys were different. We take hurt personally, when none of it is.

Give some extra grace and empathy to yourself so that you can extend that to other people. That starts with forgiveness.

First you, then anyone who has hurt you.

Become a woman who has made peace with her past—or at least can begin to. There is nothing for you there. The lessons have been learned.

Set yourself free and forgive—finally.

SAVE SOMETHING FOR YOURSELF

I know that we've talked a lot about letting love and people into your life. I want that for you. I want to see you open, flourishing, loving in ways that you may never have before.

But I can't encourage you to give up so much that you have nothing left for yourself. This may be the most important lesson that life has never taught us.

In the early pages of this book, I talked about how, as women, we've never been taught to keep ourselves. We've been taught to give it all away, because that is what women are supposed to do. We're supposed to sacrifice. Give until it hurts. Pour until we're empty.

Not us. Not anymore.

There is a time for sacrifice in life, but forgoing something temporarily for a long-term gain is different living in a constant state of depletion.

No woman of substance is poor—in any way. You should never deplete your bank account or your emotional tank, for anyone. You cannot help anyone, not even your children, from an empty place.

Let me talk to my mothers for a minute. (If you want to be a mother at some point in your life, I want you to hear this too).

You don't stop living and stop growing as a woman when you become a mother.

When women become mothers, we feel that we have to forgo everything, including our dreams.

My mother did that, and I vowed I would never do that with my daughter. Anything I have is hers, but there is a space created in my life for her and my purpose. I need my daughter to say that I loved her and that I loved people. That is the example that I am determined to set for her. That is what I want her to remember me for.

Our daughters need to see us living our dreams so they can mimic that movement and momentum in their own lives. They need to see us striving and thriving beyond surviving, so they can say, "My momma did it and I can do it too."

We want our children to say that we were not only great mothers, but that we were happy. Healthy. Loving. Energetic. Driven. Full women. Whole women.

You cannot teach what you don't do. We have to be what we want them to see.

When you tell your kids they are beautiful, you have to believe it for yourself. Children don't do what you say—they do what they see. If we want to raise beautiful, strong, resilient, loving, purpose-driven children, then we have to be all of those things in their eyes.

Earlier in the book, I talked about the peace I felt when my mother passed away. I don't remember feeling a lot of fear at all. But there was one moment that scared the living shit out of me.

Seeing her death certificate.

I'd never seen one before. I held that piece of paper in my hands and stared at it for the longest time. There was her name. The day she was born and the day she died. There was nothing significant on that piece of paper about her or her life. That paper said nothing about how much she loved her children, the dreams that she had, or what she accomplished in this world.

I would never have the chance to ask her anything else. I would never get to talk to her about the significance of her life, what she held in, where she held back, what she wished she'd done more of. I didn't know much about how she'd grown up. The things that she was afraid of or that she wished she'd tried. I had nothing to tell my daughter about the woman who raised and loved me the best that she could.

She gave away everything she had to her family. She left this earth with so much more to do, to say, to be, and to have.

She never had the opportunity to save something for herself.

Whether you are a mother or not, are you saving something for yourself? Are you saving your dreams and living them? Are you living a life of purpose? Are you saving some room for joy and fulfillment? Are you pouring into yourself?

Do you feel alive?

Don't wait until "one day" to have any of these things or to become more.

It sounds counterintuitive, but the more you save for yourself, the more you can give to everyone else.

THE POWER YOU HAVE

Becoming is moving through life as if you have unlimited power—because you do.

Femininity is a force of attraction. Men go get; women attract. That is, by nature, what we do.

We have the power of the feminine. And there is nothing greater.

Women are creatures who can create from anything. If you give us something, we create even more. You give us sperm, and we create a baby. You give us ingredients and we make a meal. You give us a house and we give you a home.

This is who we are.

You are a woman. You can command. You can require. You have this confidence, this boldness, and this power wherever you are. You can tell when an atmosphere has a feminine touch. The energy is different. They need you. We need you. Your energy is needed everywhere.

Don't be afraid to confidently and boldly express yourself. Say what you want. You will get it.

Don't be afraid to move in your power. Decide what you want. And you will have it.

Don't be afraid to show up—in any environment or in any room. Step into it. Own it.

One of the most valuable lessons that I learned as a dancer was presence. There was a power that came naturally from learning how to hold and control my body. I haven't danced professionally in more than ten years, but that presence has never left me.

Have you ever met a woman who commands a room?

It is not necessarily how she looks—it's how she carries herself. It's her presence. It's her feminine power. It's her understanding that she is a high-value woman. Just like you.

Sitting right where you are, I want you to hold your body upright. Back straight. Head up. Chest lifted.

I didn't just turn you into a dancer—I turned you into a woman who knows how to carry herself, on any stage and in any room, like the lady and queen she is.

Because becoming is presence. Becoming is power.

FEELING FEMININE

*E*very woman needs her own feminine flow rituals. These are personal practices and rituals that help you to stay grounded and connected.

You may already have some of your own, but I want to share of few of my favorites to possibly add to your list and your life:

Meditation. Meditation is a must. Even if you only have five minutes to disconnect from everything in the car, do it. Breathe. Meditation is your time to communicate with God throughout the day.

If we can snatch up the phone to call a friend to complain, then we have time to call God.

When you slow down and step away from everything, especially if you need to make a decision in the moment, you can ask yourself some guiding questions like,

"How do I feel about this?", "What do I need to say?" "Is this right?"

Take a few minutes to ask these questions, and the answers will come quickly.

. . .

FIND SOMETHING THAT YOU LOVE. I love red roses. For me, roses symbolize so many things. Strength. Love. Beauty. So, I have them everywhere, as much as I can. I buy roses regularly. I do rose petal facials. I drink rose teas and rose lattes. My grandmother's name was Rose, so that's my daughter's middle name. I surround myself with roses to keep my spirit lifted and to feel happy.

Find something that you love and keep it close. If you love flowers, then flowers it is. If it's a certain scent, color, or coffee, buy more of that and make it a constant in your life. Light your life up with something special to you to remind yourself that you are loved.

Feed your soul. When problems pop up, don't deal with them right away. Step back, get into the space of feeling good, and come back to it.

What would feel good to you at the moment? For me, sometimes it's a glass of wine or spending some time playing with my daughter. Yours could be taking a walk outside, calling a good girlfriend to just laugh, or dancing to some music that makes you feel sexy.

Feed your mind. Your body needs food and so does your mind. Teach yourself what you don't know. Seek knowledge in books and courses. Read things that help you to learn more about yourself and that inspire and awaken things inside of you. Then go deeper than reading and listening. Start applying and practicing the principles that you learn. Put your knowledge to work.

Feel beautiful. I keep my nails, toes, and eyebrows done. I wear flowy fabrics, ruffles, and skirts. I have my own jewelry line, so I always have some of my bracelets on. Red is my power color, so I wear matte red lipstick almost every day. These seem like small things, but I've found them to make all the difference for me as a woman. I've learned that femininity is an energy that we can channel.

As the inside of me softened and started to heal, and as I became more open to love, my exterior needed to soften too.

I want people to see the blessings on me, to see and feel God on me. When I feel beautiful, I notice a shift in the people around me.

When people are in your presence, they should feel something different about you. Decide what it is that makes you feel beautiful—

your lipstick, clothes, scent, jewelry, whatever it is—and put it on all the time.

Stay in the space of money. Find ways to feel abundant. Money is energy, so when you want to increase, you have to be around it. Go to it. Have high-value conversations. Touch money. Give money away. Find ways to increase.

And let me say this—you don't have to push. Nothing happens smoothly when you push. You are in flow. Whatever you want and need will come easily. Work your plans, yes. But you don't need to force anything. Find the flow and stay in it.

Keep a beautiful home. You want a home that feels warm and is always in a loving state. Do what you need to do to cultivate that energy. Feng shui is a beautiful practice to bring into your home. Surround your home with what feels like love to you. Keep it clean and clear of negativity. It will make all the difference in your life.

YOU DID IT

⤜⤛

MY LOVE LETTER TO YOU

*W*ow, you really made it through the book! How do you feel? Are you enlightened? I hope so.

This book was designed to reveal YOU to yourself, not to tell you anything new. This book assists you in creating your desired life, while gaining an understanding and a growth mindset through this journey of womanhood. The beautiful part about this journey is that you're already whole. I wanted to shed light on my journey as a demonstration that our lives are made up of personal choices, boundaries, and goal setting. I wish I had a safe space to have these conversations growing up. I would have saved a little more energy.

Today, we have so many tools in the palms of our hands. Yet, the resources seem so distant. I wanted to ensure that each page was full of potent content. Direct information alongside tools, affirming words, self-reflection questions, and reflective space. The things that you need to set you on your journey to becoming the woman you want to be.

My goal was to get to the point. This is serious business. There is a restructuring process that is needed to peel back the layers of the person you have been to this day. The woman you are today is not the end destination. There is some more work to do.

This guide was intended to shake you up. Get you asking those tough self-evolution questions. You may have a lot of questions in your head right now, but there are two that I want you to consider answering first:

1. **What do I want?**
2. **Does that feel good to me?**

These are the questions that I use to guide my life every day. Every decision, big and small, comes down to these two things. If we can be clear about what we really want, and use our spirits to confirm that we are on the right path to having it, then we can't go wrong. This is why we have to become intimate with ourselves. Get real with ourselves.

Becoming intimate with yourself is to have those no BS conversations about your Blessings, your Boundaries and Becoming the woman you are designed to be. All of that starts with you. It's time to tap in and find your strength in your femininity. I am definitely here for women's empowerment, but motivation/ inspiration and application are separate things. Got damn it feels great to be sexy, feminine, and powerful! There is so much power in your femininity! And it all starts with your mindset. There is a woman who is all of those things —sexy, feminine, and powerful—inside of you.

Are you afraid to meet her?

You see how I did that? I want to get deeper. You run deep and the only way to tap into that space is to reveal YOU to YOU. I want you to stop and take a long look around yourself. As a matter of fact, do it right now. Is everything and everyone in your life purposeful? Do your surroundings uplift you? Sniff the air. Is it your desired scent? How are you fueling your body? Where is your energy? What are you attracting? Do you feel God's presences on you? Ask yourself these questions. And if the answer to any of them is, "No," you have the power to shift everything around you.

Let me remind you, our life is not about perfection, it is about constant correction. None of us have it figured out. I am here to assure you of God's purpose. We are striving to make women whole. In spirit, physically, emotionally and financially. YES! You cannot give from an empty space. It is a sin to be broke. How can you go through this journey not showing up as your best? This is why you need to get into yourself, your whole self, so that you can give to the world. Your family needs you. Women need you. The world needs you.

Together, we are elevating the game. *Elevating the whole woman.*

You will never think the same after this book. The synchronicities are going to show up fast because once you become enlightened, you are now responsible for the information that you now hold. You will be wiser in understanding your blessings, creating loving boundaries, and, with that combination, naturally, you are going to BE present in your journey. You are the creator. You have free will.

God has a plan for us, and because you picked up this book, I guess you can assume that you are in alignment with your purpose. Congratulations in advance on what you are about to accomplish! Now go out and live and be intentional.

LOVE,
    Fantajia DeLisa

A SELF-REFLECTION JOURNAL

𝕭OUNDARIES
What are the new standards that you are setting for yourself?

WHAT BOUNDARIES ARE you creating based on those standards?

WHAT RELATIONSHIPS or areas in your life do need to set better boundaries?

WHAT IS YOUR DESIRED LIFESTYLE? and what do you have to say No to, to achieve your goal?

WHAT ARE your strengths around boundaries?

WHAT ARE your opportunities with setting boundaries?

. . .

BLESSINGS

What are you believing God for?

WRITE OUT A PRAYER TO GOD, expressing what you are believing Him for.

WHAT DAILY PRACTICES will you put in place to stay in the spirit of what you are believing for?

WHERE ARE YOU ALREADY SUCCESSFUL?

LIST 10 AFFIRMATIONS you will use in your life going forward to help keep your blessings at the front of your life?

List 3 new Scriptures you will stand on?

BECOMING

Who are you becoming? Write out the vision for that woman.

WHAT CHANGES CAN you make in your life and in your home to reflect this woman?

WHAT IS your purpose on this earth right now? (This area continues to change daily, but is in alignment with the bigger goal.)

. . .

WHAT IS YOUR BIG DREAM? What does it look like, smell like and feel like? Get up in your dream.

BREAK the Goal down into sections.

What are the goals that you need to set for yourself to achieve that dream?

ON A SCALE OF 1-10, how much do you love yourself?

If your score is a 5 or below, why do you feel that way?

What experiences made you feel less than?

WHAT DO you need to finally forgive yourself for?

Who do you need to forgive?

Write them a letter and burn it.

ABOUT THE AUTHOR

A powerhouse speaker, mentor, and entrepreneur, Fantajia DeLisa Thomas is here to help every woman she meets to feel lifted and loved. Known for her magnetic presence, the classically trained dancer will tell anyone who listens that it was God, grit, and grace that has given her the life and success she has. Now with a national stage, she has decided to rise with women and use her testimony to enlighten women and show them how to tap into that same power to reclaim who they were designed to be.

www.ingramcontent.com/pod-product-compliance
Lightning Source LLC
LaVergne TN
LVHW051416080426
835508LV00022B/3116